THE
LAND BEFORE US
The Making of Ancient Alberta

THE ROYAL TYRRELL MUSEUM OF PALAEONTOLOGY

RED DEER COLLEGE PRESS

Discovery Books are published by
Red Deer College Press
56 Avenue & 32 Street
Box 5005
Red Deer Alberta Canada T4N 5H5

Designed by Kunz & Associates Limited. Printed and bound in Korea for Red Deer College Press.

The publishers gratefully acknowledge the financial assistance of the Alberta Foundation for the Arts, the Canada Council, the Department of Communications and Red Deer College.

COMMITTED TO THE DEVELOPMENT OF CULTURE AND THE ARTS

Canadian Cataloguing in Publication Data
Main entry under title:
The Land before us
(Discovery Books)
Includes index.
ISBN 0-88995-118-7 (bound.)
ISBN 0-88995-123-3 (pbk.)
1. Geology–Alberta–History. I. Tyrrell Museum of Palaeontology. II. Series: Discovery Books (Red Deer, Alta.)
QE186.L36 1994   557.123   C94-910305-5

Contents

FOREWORD

This colourful account of Alberta's palaeontological history instills in each of us a sense of pride in the scientific accomplishments of the Royal Tyrrell Museum. *The Land Before Us* is about Alberta's past, yet it reinforces our commitment to the future. The educational research represented in this book reflects the government's commitment to investing in people and ideas. *The Land Before Us* will be an important and respected educational resource.

Gary G. Mar
Minister
Alberta Community Development

Unravelling the creation of our province is an exciting and never-ending scientific study. Alberta has been drowned by salty seas, baked under subtropical suns and crushed beneath tons of ice. Life has endured through all these changes—constantly evolving. The Royal Tyrrell Museum's scientific mandate is to investigate and explain the history of life on this planet, especially as it relates to Alberta. Palaeontology is not just about dead things—it is a dynamic changing science that brings the past to life.

The Land Before Us presents the prehistoric development of Alberta and the Western Interior of North America. We hope to communicate the excitement of the past to Albertans of today, showing how the resources and life we take for granted came to be. The Tyrrell's scientists can be proud of their role in the discovery of our province's past.

Bruce G. Naylor
Director
Royal Tyrrell Museum of Palaeontology

ACKNOWLEDGEMENTS

The Royal Tyrrell Museum of Palaeontology and Red Deer College Press gratefully acknowledge Renaissance Energy Ltd. as the major sponsor of *The Land Before Us*.

The Royal Tyrrell Museum also thanks the Canadian Geological Foundation of the Geological Association of Canada, the Canadian Society of Petroleum Geologists and the Cooperating Society of the Royal Tyrrell Museum for their support.

The Land Before Us was originally conceived by scientists at the Royal Tyrrell Museum of Palaeontology. The concept evolved under the influence of a team of scientists, artists, writers and designers. Dr. David Eberth acted as scientific advisor for all text and artwork. With the generous support of Renaissance Energy Ltd., Dennis Budgen served as artistic advisor and produced the cover and chapter-opening illustrations. Other artwork by Dennis Budgen, David Eberth, Val Herman, Patrick Hurst, Vladimr Krb, Donna Sloan and Jan Sovak is used throughout. Parks Canada graciously provided the Burgess Shale reconstruction.

Photographs were provided by Dennis Braman, Robert Campbell, Clive Coy, Phil Currie, David Eberth, Mach II, NASA, Collin Orthner, Donna Sloan, Susan Swibald, Ole Tenold, and Michael Todor Fine Photography.

Andrew Nikiforuk served as writer and editor. The book was designed by Ben Kunz. Monty Reid, Dennis Johnson and Bruce Naylor kept the project on track. Linda Reynolds and Rick Thomas provided assistance in earlier phases of the project. The title was suggested by Tim Bird.

SUPPORTERS

The Royal Tyrrell Museum of Paleontology gratefully acknowledges the ongoing support of the Museum's Cooperating Society, whose generous assistance made the publication possible.

Renaissance Energy Ltd. and the Canadian Geological Foundation made important contributions that sustained the development of this book.

Many other contributors also supported the project. Our thanks go to the following:
Brian Cooley Sculpture & Design Co.
Canadian Society of Petroleum Geologists
Chauvco Resources Ltd.
Corexcana Ltd.
Enron Oil Canada Ltd.
Graham Davies Geological Consultants Ltd.
Pan-Alberta Gas Ltd.
Resman Oil & Gas Ltd.
Sabre Energy Ltd.
Total Petroleum Ltd.

Thank you all for helping to put *The Land Before Us* before us.

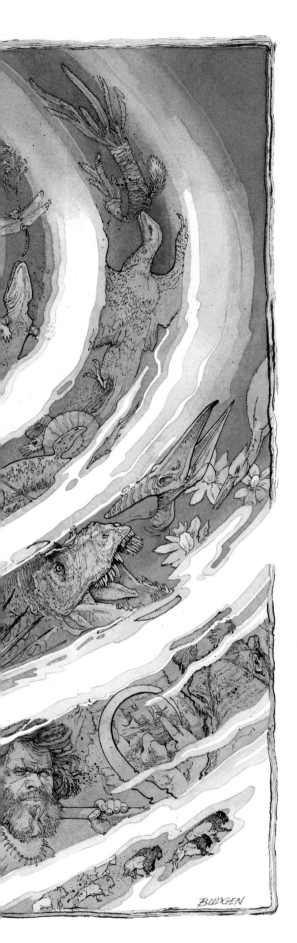

Introduction

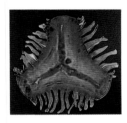

Magnified a thousand times, this fossilized spore speaks of Alberta's ancient land environments.

Alberta is a richly diverse land where rolling parkland loses itself in boreal forests and where shortgrass prairie abruptly butts up against the hard feet of rocky mountains.

Every place forces upon its people different adaptations and attitudes, and one of the most persistent beliefs among the province's citizens is that the land is new. Like most westerners, Albertans assume, if not hope, that they inhabit an embryonic place that is still making its way in the scheme of things.

Geologists and palaeontologists, however, tell a radically different story. Having read the province's rocks and fossils, they know that Alberta is solidly part of the earth's four and a half billion-year-old history. The land before us has witnessed immense floods, great oceans, volcanic eruptions, asteroid bombardments, bacterial armies, evolutionary oddballs, reef builders, towering glaciers and a wild assortment of plants and animals. Alberta, too, may have witnessed the coming of humans to North America. As a part and partner to creation, Alberta is a well-rooted place and not new at all; in fact, its land and rocks speak

7

Contrasting scenes: Alberta's current grasslands, such as this landscape near Rumsey (above), gently hint of Cenozoic plains grazed by ancient mammals (below).

directly to ancient doings, some incontestable and some mysterious.

This book tells Alberta's ancient biological and physical history—an amazing and still unfinished chronicle that scientists add to and subtract from as they uncover and study more rocks and fossils. *The Land Before Us* properly begins with the making of the planet just before the Precambrian Eon some 4.6 billion years ago and ends with the trappings of civilization on the plains during the Cenozoic, an era spanning from sixty-five million years ago to the present.

The vastness of geological time sketched here can be daunting. The first chapter covers roughly eighty-five percent of the earth's history while the remaining chapters deal with the last fifteen percent. Standing on the banks of the Milk or Peace River on a starry autumn night, it is easy to imagine the immensity of space. But the senses have difficulty perceiving the vastness of geological time without reference to a scale.

During the last 230 years, geologists have developed and refined a calendar that breaks down the passage of vast amounts of time into

Millions of Years Ago	Eon	Era	Period	Epoch
			Quaternary	Holocene
1.7				Pleistocene
		C E N O Z O I C	Tertiary	Pliocene
				Miocene
				Oligocene
				Eocene
				Palaeocene
65	P H A N E R O Z O I C	M E S O Z O I C	Cretaceous	
140			Jurassic	
210			Triassic	
250			Permian	
290		P A L A E O Z O I C	Carboniferous	
360			Devonian	
410			Silurian	
440			Ordovician	
500			Cambrian	
590				
	P R E C A M B R I A N	PROTEROZOIC		
2,500		ARCHEAN		
4,000		HADEAN		
4,600				

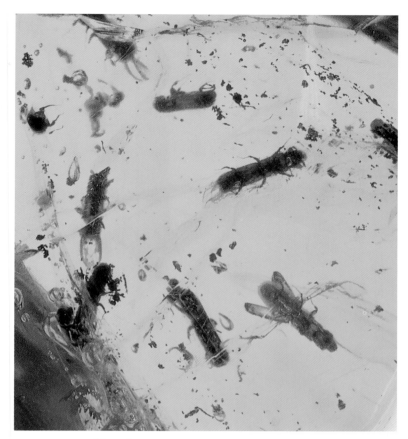

more manageable (if not more imaginable) eons, eras, periods and epochs. In their first attempts to build a geological time scale, some geologists recognized that trilobites lived before dinosaurs and that dinosaurs lived before humans. As such, they were able to place fossils in a relative order from oldest to youngest but without really knowing how much time was involved. At the turn of the century, radiometric dating began to correct this vagueness, and palaeontologists, the students of ancient life, can now tell with greater accuracy when the rocks and their fossil treasures were laid down.

In addition to faithfully recording the immensity of Alberta's age, this book presents evolution as accepted scientific fact. In the eyes of a geologist or palaeontologist, evolution refers to cumulative changes in the genetic makeup of groups of organisms, which eventually affect the way they look and act. Such mutations may strengthen, diminish or exert no influence at all on a group's chances of survival and its members' ability to reproduce more of their kind.

The geological time scale (left) is a calendar documenting the longest succession of events in Earth history.

Trapped in amber and later found in a coal deposit near Taber, Alberta, these primitive biting flies (above) lived more than seventy-five million years ago.

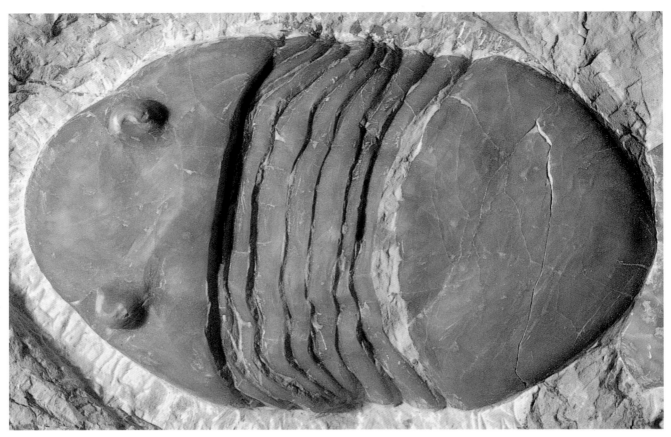

Any object that records ancient life more than ten thousand years old, whether it be the remains of a trilobite (above) or the footprint of a dinosaur (below), qualifies as a fossil.

Evolution is not a conscious act among organisms. It operates on populations over many generations. It is something left to the complex and sometimes random relationships that develop between living things and their given homes, climates and companions.

Alberta's geological history often shows evolution as the survival of the lucky or a game of opportunity rather than an ongoing battle between competitors.

Extinction is very much a part of evolution's process. Ninety-nine percent of all the

The toothy skull of a *Tyrannosaurus rex* (left) and the skin imprint of a hadrosaur (below) attest to the land's remarkable history.

organisms that ever inhabited the planet are gone. Some scientists have even suggested that mass extinctions take place, on average, every twenty-six million years as a result of asteroid bombardments or other otherworldly phenomena. Most of the famous and infamous creatures that once prowled Alberta, including tyrannosaurs and stromatoporoids, have long since disappeared. Geological history often reads like an ongoing drama in which old lives pass away and new lives take their place.

Although this book contains Latin names and detailed time scales, readers don't need a university degree to understand it. In *The Land Before Us,* scientists at the Royal Tyrrell Museum of Palaeontology share, in everyday language, the great and little-understood stories about the making of Earth and a unique political geography called Alberta.

If this book invites readers to think of Jurassic collisions when they view the Rockies, to imagine Devonian seas when they travel the prairies and to picture Cretaceous swamps when they camp in Dinosaur Provincial Park, then it will have achieved its modest purpose—the restoration of memory in an ancient and fabulous land.

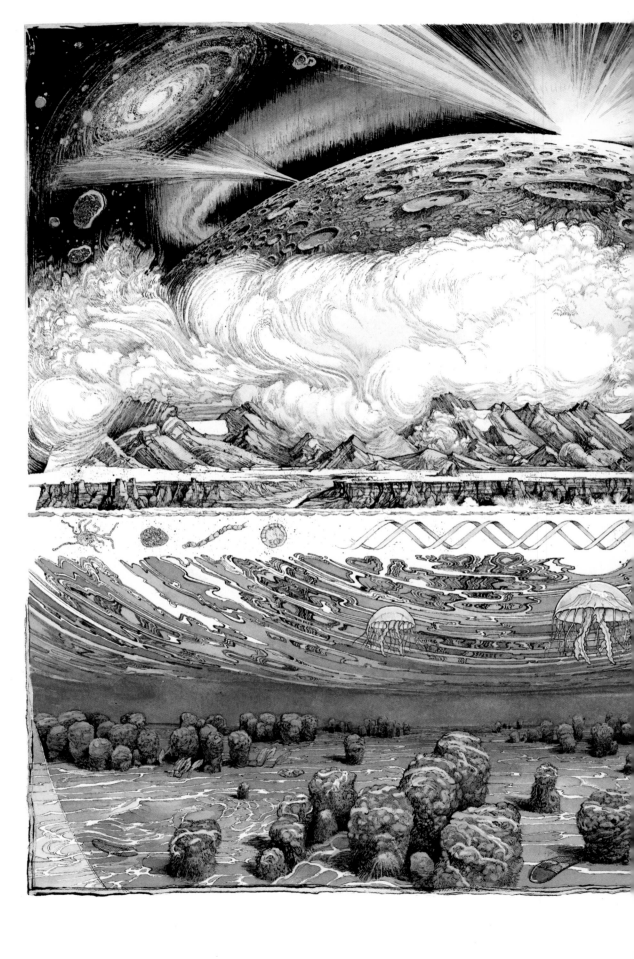

Chapter One

A Precambrian Genesis

This modern algal mound, or stromatolite, from Shark Bay, Australia, is almost identical to its two-billion-year-old predecessors. Ancient stromatolites have become Alberta's oldest fossils.

In the beginning, say the Blackfoot, the world was nothing but water. Whether by design or boredom, Old Man, the Blackfoot creator, got curious about this state of affairs and sent some animals below to find what lay beneath the surface. A duck, an otter and a badger dived into the depths but found nothing. Finally, Old Man sent a muskrat, which returned with a small ball of mud. Old Man grabbed the ooze and breathed life into it until the mud ball ballooned into the shape of the earth.

Then Old Man set to work. He piled up rocks to make mountains and dug great gouges in the land to make rivers and lakes. He covered the ground with bundles of trees and mats of grasses. He made all kinds of fish, birds and animals. And with a lump of clay he even fashioned himself a pretty wife. Together they created a people that would eventually become one of the most flamboyant Indian cultures on the Great Plains.

In contrast to the Blackfoot version of genesis, modern scientists tell a longer and more complicated story. They make no mention of Old Man, but their version is also rich in

With a fiery explosion aptly known as the Big Bang, the universe came into existence some fourteen and a half billion years ago.

poetry and drama. The scientific account begins some fourteen and a half billion years ago when all matter and energy now in existence was released with a "Big Bang." Almost ten billion years later, the Solar System took embryonic shape as an immense and heated cloud of stardust. Driven by the sheer force of gravity, this solar nebula eventually imploded, releasing the force of untold thermonuclear reactions that created the sun, the giver of light, energy and ultimately life.

Hadean Earth

In the great dark space of the new Solar System, gases and other dust particles swirled. Drawn together by their own gravitational forces, they gradually coalesced to form the planets. Earth was among them. Thanks to the sun's gravitational pull, the planets banded together into orbits rather than floating off as bits of cosmic waste. As the sun ignited its long stable burn, it sent violent solar winds across the Solar System. These winds swept the system clean of remnant

stardust and other debris, and blew out a primitive atmosphere of hydrogen, carbon, nitrogen and ammonia from the nascent Earth.

Primitive Earth resembled a Blackfoot mud ball and, as some early geologists imagined, smelled very much like the Greek underworld, Hades. This explains why scientists now refer to this period as the Hadean Era. Meteorites the size of mountains pockmarked a steaming planet whose atmosphere reeked of poisonous formaldehyde and cyanide. As the forceful addition of extraterrestrial material expanded the girth of the earth, its temperature rose. Iron and nickel, already a part of the earth's makeup, melted and flowed into the centre of the earth, forming a dense planetary core. (Although thirty-five percent of the earth's mass is iron, only eight percent of this metal can now be found near the planet's surface.) As this central hot spot grew in size and intensity, the entire planet collapsed into a ball of molten rock.

Over four hundred million years, magma on the surface cooled, forming a thin and uncertain crust less than fifty kilometres thick. Today, the tallest mountains and deepest ocean floors are all part of this crust. Even so, if the earth were the size of an apple, the earth's fragile outer layer would be thinner than the apple's skin.

Beneath the crust lies an intermediate and much hotter layer known as the mantle. In Hadean times, hot rock from the mantle continually seeped through the crust to create great pools and volcanic eruptions. As lava spilled onto the surface, cooler rock sank to the earth's fiery depths to be reheated. In this manner, giant currents of ponderous magma, known as convection cells, began to stir around the planet, tearing the crust into a number of great plates the size of continents.

Propelled by subterranean forces, these plates moved gradually in a conveyor-belt-like fashion as oceans of magma flowed beneath. The first slow and steamy waltz of continents took place about three billion years ago. Where plates collided, mountain belts, earthquakes and volcanoes appeared, and where they pulled apart, earthquakes, deep rifts and molten rock flowed in their wake. Californians know all too well that these not-so-subtle plate movements continue.

At the same time that the plates formed and continents began to drift, the earth's ancestral atmosphere began to brew. A continual meteor bombardment, along with gases and vapours released by the spewing of hot rock, resulted in sizeable collections of carbon dioxide, hydrogen and methane. Although still a deadly

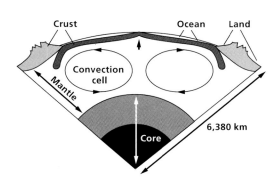

mixture by human standards, this gaseous cocktail prepared the way for Earth's first life.

As the bleak surface of the new planet continued to cool over several million years, clouds of water vapour turned into torrential rains. Unlike its sister planets, Earth was far enough away from the sun to prevent its water from evaporating and close enough to keep the precious liquid from freezing. Soon, great oceans formed, geysers boiled and earthbound asteroids plummeted toward watery depths. If Alberta existed during this geological era, it consisted of fetal rock on some unnamed island continent in a primordial ocean. Save for some Australian mineral crystals, no known rocks of this age exist anywhere on Earth. There, too, was no life.

Archean Murks

During the Archean Era, from four to two and a half billion years ago, life did not so much arise as it did stew in a landscape of deep oceans, bubbling ponds and mineral-rich

Earth's early atmosphere (above) was a smelly and noxious mixture of gases.

The earth (left) is made up of a double-layered metal-rich core, a layer of molten rock called the mantle and a thin crust of hard rock that is divided into tectonic plates. Currents in the molten rock drive plate motions, causing giant rifts where plates separate, or mountains and volcanoes where plates collide.

Precambrian rocks are
visible only in the Rockies
and the northeast (right).

lakes. Scientists suspect that the carbon-rich, or organic, compounds needed to start life accumulated in several ways. Meteorites, which still harbour amino acids and other molecular hitchhikers, could very well have seeded the earth's incubatory waters with life or its essential ingredients.

But Nature's own laboratory may have induced its own chemical reactions by subjecting the emerging land to cycles of heat and cold, light and dark, drought and rain. Blinding lightning storms even furnished a steady supply of electricity. Since the 1950s, scientists have successfully created organic molecules in their labs by simulating Nature's ancient open-air experiments. To do so, they simply run electrical currents through water vapour, nitrogen, carbon dioxide, carbon monoxide, methane and ammonia.

Over millions of years, new molecules created by Nature or introduced by meteors stuck to gooey muds and clays in the earth's oceans. Crowded together in such environments, they learned to join or split into more molecules without destroying themselves. These earliest forms of life, the humblest of the humble, didn't have cell walls and depended upon other organic compounds in their midst for nutrients.

From this simple beginning, a variety of bacterial microbes emerged to colonize the planet. The daily life of ancient bacteria consisted of eating hydrogen sulphide, secreting sulphur, multiplying and then eating again. Death came abruptly with meteorite blasts or volcanic eruptions. But such interruptions didn't deter bacteria from overrunning the earth. Some speedy bacteria, for instance, can swell up and split in two every twenty minutes. This means that in half a day, one microbe can make more of itself than all of the number of Albertans who have ever lived. Hardy microbes in the shapes of rods and spheres slowly invented a number of useful processes, ranging from fermentation to photosynthesis, that have made the earth hospitable.

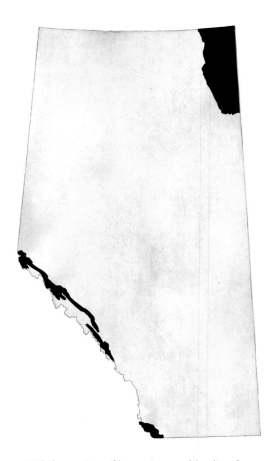

While armies of bacteria greedily dined on hydrogen sulphide, blue and green microbes called proalgae learned how to consume carbon dioxide. Unlike their bacterial cousins, proalgae had the ability to use energy from the sun's light rays to split carbon dioxide into carbon and oxygen, a gas toxic to most other microbial life. But as the proalgae multiplied, they produced oxygen in ever greater quantities, creating the earth's first great pollution crisis, or what biologist Lynn Margulis eloquently calls "the Oxygen holocaust."

Oxygen can be a ruthless burner, or "oxidizer," of unprotected compounds such as iron or manganese. Not surprisingly, the first wave of the pollutant was captured by iron molecules in ocean mud where it was safely locked away as rust-coloured iron oxide. But when the ocean's iron-rich sediments could no longer hold more oxygen, the radical gas began building up in ocean waters and in the atmosphere. Whereas some life-forms retreated to areas where oxygen was in low supply, like the ocean

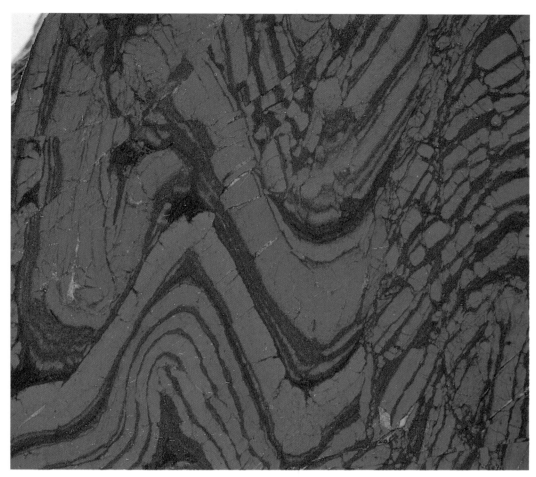

Alternating layers of red and grey in banded rock from Lake Superior (left) speak of accumulating oxygen in the earth's atmosphere.

depths, others developed membranes to fend off the gas. Eventually, some forms modified the machinery of cellular metabolism and began to breathe the once-deadly gas.

While hyperactive teams of bacteria performed their good work, ancestral Alberta took shape in bits and pieces. During the Archean Era, North America looked like an unassembled puzzle scattered over three separate island continents. Parts of the deep crust near Drumheller and Lake Athabasca, which today lie 21 kilometres below the ground, formed the tips of two of these continents while a deep crustal segment near Medicine Hat sat forlornly on another island.

Alberta's oldest surface rocks date back to this period some 2.8 billion years ago and lie near the Slave River in the northeastern corner of the province. The igneous rock there forms part of the Canadian Shield, a great mass of Archean scripture from which geologists read much of the world's early history. The

Northwest Territories, by the way, are home to Earth's most ancient rock–tonalite gneiss, more than a billion years older than Alberta's Archean collection.

In the earth's perpetual rearrangement of continents, parts of North America (including Alberta) moved hundreds of kilometres over millions of years, leading to various collisions, unions and separations. In fact, the world's existing continents have banded together to form a giant supercontinent at least four times in the last two and a half billion years, only to be torn apart again. One such supercontinental union took place nearly two billion years ago. This landmass, including much of Alberta's foundations, lay along the equator.

Proterozoic Ploddings

High noon in the Proterozoic Era came when the supercontinent divorced, and Alberta's western borders slowly became beach-front property. This event occurred about 1.7 billion

Two-billion-year-old stromatolite fossils found in Alberta are identical to living species now found in Australia (right).

The Purcell Group dominates parts of Waterton National Park (below).

years ago. Scientists speculate that a narrow sea or huge lake flooded the supercontinent as the breakup began. Antarctica and Australia probably faced Alberta across this body of water. At the time, Calgary-to-be sat amidst blowing sand just 240 kilometres from the seashore. While the continents continued to drift apart over a four-hundred-million-year period, the combined efforts of water and wind left a great deal of sediment along Alberta's ancient coastline. The magnificent red and green mountains in Waterton Lakes National Park, known to geologists as the Purcell Group, bear testament to this rock layering.

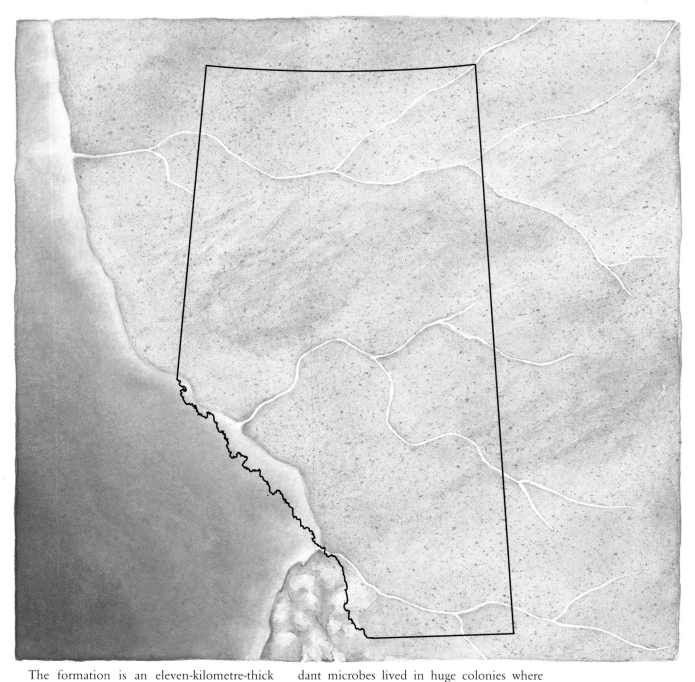

The formation is an eleven-kilometre-thick sandwich of sandstone, slate, shale, volcanic rock and limestone.

During the Proterozoic, Alberta was likely a balmy but barren place with tropical temperatures. Nameless rivers as wide as the Athabasca flowed across the land and poured into a nameless ocean along the province's western shore. According to ripple marks, mud cracks and salt crystals on the Purcell rocks, coastal water levels rose and fell.

The first primitive Albertans, proalgae, appeared in shallow coastal pools. These abundant microbes lived in huge colonies where they lived and died on top of each other. Shaped like giant cabbages or foot stools, these colonies, called stromatolites, rose up to ten metres in height and dominated much of the earth's shorelines. The Purcell rocks dutifully preserve the remains of these fossilized castles. Living stromatolites, in fact, can still be found in western Australia and the Persian Gulf.

While microbes manned their stromatolite ramparts, more and more primitive life-forms took advantage of the atmosphere's growing supply of oxygen. About one and a half to

Proterozoic Alberta: A barren and rocky land with expansive shorelines.

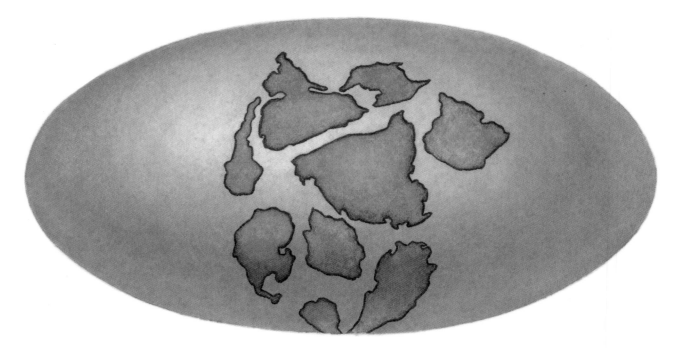

A continental puzzle: One billion years ago, North America occupied an uncertain middle position while Australia and Antarctica pulled away toward the north-west (above).

Rocks of the Windermere Supergroup (below) are exposed around Lake Louise and Jasper, where they form slabs of grey slate.

two billion years ago, a new oxygen breather, the eukaryotic cell, evolved complete with a nucleus that housed all of its reproductive software. In dramatic fossil evidence, the much larger and more complex eukaryotes look so different from bacteria that it's almost as if a Model T Ford had been followed by a Batmobile. The eukaryotes' debut, however, brought welcome diversity to Alberta's bacterial monopoly.

As the eukaryotes assembled all the bits and pieces of the modern cell, some lost their ability to use photosynthesis as a dining tool. Some became parasites while others became predators, eating other cells for food. From these early eukaryote cells, all plant and animal life as Albertans know it bravely evolved. In the process, the eukaryotes bid goodbye to the bacterial fraternity that made their emergence possible.

Between 1.2 billion and 760 million years ago another supercontinent formed only to drift southward. It, too, pulled apart, sending South America and Africa on their separate journeys. When Antarctica and Australia finally broke away for good, the Pacific Ocean rushed into being, placing Alberta at the salty edge of a newly shaped North America.

To geologists, large recognizable packages of rock come in groups or supergroups. Alberta's Pacific days are well recorded in the Windermere Supergroup, a collection of rock that stretches along the Rocky Mountains. Windermere's rocky book consists of a mixture of pebbles, sandstones, shales and limestones that

weather and glaciers, over time, abandoned on the Pacific sea floor about 760 to 600 million years ago. The rocks tell of several big rivers that crisscrossed Alberta, dumping their silt and sand into the Pacific. They reveal that stromatolite mounds now had the company of jellyfish creatures the size of coffee cups. Worm-shaped animals and ferns also bobbed up and down the coastline. Scientists really don't know much about these odd-shaped blobs except that they all shared an important characteristic—none had shells or skeletons.

The Windermere rocks also record a major advance of glaciers. This ice age froze much of the earth with the odd exception of Antarctica and Siberia, which at the time lay comfortably near the equator. The Windermere arrangement of huge boulders mixed with fine-grained silt and sand speaks directly of the behaviour of ice. When a glacier melts, it bombs the floors of ocean bays with heavy baggage in the form of big rocks. What makes the Windermere Supergroup so distinct is that its rock package contains all the debris of an ice age as well as the fossils of stromatolites and other soft-bodied creatures that cavorted in warm water. One explanation of this unique juxtaposition is that icebergs floated southward from colder climes only to melt as they passed Alberta's coast.

The Windermere Supergroup commemorates Alberta's infancy on Earth as a bare place with a nice shoreline and little life. The quiet stillness of its Precambrian cradle, however, would soon give way to a strange parade of creatures big and small, some of which looked as if they emerged from a bizarre hallucination.

Floating and anchored jellyfishlike creatures the size of coffee cups lived at the edges of Precambrian seas among mounds of stromatolites.

Chapter Two

The Early Palaeozoic

At the age of fifty-nine, Charles Doolittle Walcott, one of America's great palaeontologists, discovered the Burgess Shale in British Columbia.

In 1909, Charles Doolittle Walcott, a prominent American scientist, discovered a mother lode of fossils stamped on one of Canada's ancient seabeds. The legendary geologist, then secretary of the Smithsonian Institute, stumbled upon the find high in the Canadian Rockies near Field, British Columbia. The rich quarry, no longer than a city block, has since yielded tens of thousands of wonderfully detailed fossils on slabs of shale.

Having spent much of his life tracking trilobites and Precambrian stromatolites, Walcott recognized the wonderful little beasts, which he hammered, chiseled and dynamited out of the Burgess Shale over a period of nine years, as "the finest collection ... I have ever seen." What he didn't realize was that he had found a special moment in history when the diversity of basic body types as anatomically distinct as comic-book aliens was far greater than it would ever be again.

The Burgess creatures that flourished off what was then Canada's west coast reflect what palaeontologists properly call "the Cambrian explosion." This event, which happened 570

No longer than a city block, the Burgess Shale is located halfway up Mt. Field, British Columbia (above).

Athabasca Falls cuts through quartzites of the Gog Group (below).

rated the beginning of the Palaeozoic Era, which spans 320 million years. Because so much happened during this time, geologists divide the Palaeozoic into a dynamic six-pack: Cambrian, Ordovician, Silurian, Devonian, Carboniferous and Permian. These periods, each of which represents the passage of thirty to ninety million years, witnessed the repeated flooding and drying of Alberta, mass extinctions and the slow and persistent colonization of land by plants and animals.

But even before the Burgess creatures that scuttled about Alberta's coastal waters appeared, the province's landscape was evolving. Lifeless rivers poured into the Pacific while winds swept barren and rocky ground. The tonnes of sand and mud that eventually clouded Pacific waters are now mutely displayed as red and pink quartzites of the Gog Group found at Athabasca Falls, south of Jasper.

In the early Cambrian, the western margin of North America lay along the equator, facing outward on a newly born Pacific Ocean. The modern border of British Columbia and Alberta marked the edge of the continent. North America, which was drifting toward the east, had been rotated clockwise so that what is now the west coast actually looked north. No

million years ago, celebrates the advent of creatures armed with shells and skeletons, or animals with hard parts, in the fossil record. Although the Burgess collection dates forty million years after this event, it faithfully presents a wonderful window on the results: fearsome and odd-looking worms, jellyfish and crablike beasts with poetic names like *Canadaspis, Wiwaxia, Hallucigenia* and *Anomalocaris*. As the geologist Stephen Jay Gould recently wrote, the Burgess Shale is really "our sole vista upon the inception of modern life in all its fullness."

The Cambrian explosion properly inaugu-

Early Palaeozoic Alberta: Beach-front property facing the Pacific.

collisions or mountain building would occur for another two hundred million years or so.

Following North America's separation from Antarctica and Australia at the end of the Precambrian, the western fringes of the continent began to sink. As Alberta continued to erode and flatten out, the seas gradually moved inland. Eventually, over a course of 180 million years, shallow oceans completely drowned Alberta, leaving only small parts of North America high and dry. During the Cambrian and early Ordovician periods, the sea worked like a determined army, advancing and retreating more than ten times, each time gaining more ground. By the beginning of the Ordovician Period, water had claimed all of southern Alberta as well as parts of Saskatchewan and Manitoba. To the native-born of the prairies, the land still whispers of these long-forgotten oceans.

The first respite Alberta got from all this watering occurred during the middle of the Ordovician Period when the northern side of the continent began to collide with Greenland and western Europe. This geological event lifted the land, spilling the seas out of western Canada for about twenty million years. But

At the beginning of the Palaeozoic, geologic forces rotated North America clockwise so that it lay along the equator well separated from sister landmasses.

by the end of the Ordovician Period, the waters returned, this time submerging almost the entire continent.

Unlike the modern-day Pacific, with its deep and cool waters, the seas that covered Alberta and North America were shallow, measuring only hundreds of metres in depth. These warm seas harboured a vast number of shellfish, sponges and primitive corals as well as a variety of algae. Over time, suspended limey muds carpeted the sea floor and gave the water a blue-green tint like that of the Caribbean.

Currents sculpted these calcium-rich sediments into shifting mounds or shoals on the sea floor. Along the continent's western edge, where the shallow seas dropped off in the deep blue of the Pacific, extensive reefs formed, encouraged by the upwelling of deep nutrient-rich waters. Composed of a mixture of bottom-dwelling invertebrates and algae, these reefs had a stability that limey shoals didn't. Over time, some reefs formed collections of islands and submerged barriers all along the coast. During periodic drops in sea levels, silts and clays from eroded landscapes would be carried seaward to coat reefs and shoals.

When the Rocky Mountains rose in the Mesozoic and Cenozoic, they exposed the ancient layers of limestone and shale deposited in the Palaeozoic seas of British Columbia and Alberta. One of the most spectacular views of early Palaeozoic rocks is along the Banff-Jasper highway where the vertical cliff-forming walls of Cambrian rock form the scarps of Castle Mountain. The subtle differences in the colour and style of weathering of the rock layers that make up these mountains actually reflect the different environments of the Cambrian and Ordovician seas. Thus, parts of Castle Mountain are made up of different layers that reflect ancient reef and limey shoal deposits (the Cathedral, Eldon and Waterfowl formations) while other layers represent mud and shale deposits derived from coastal lowlands that were exposed during brief retreats of the sea (the Stephen, Pika, Arctomys and Sullivan formations).

Hard Parts

Of all the milestones that early Palaeozoic rock so patiently records, the most dear to palaeontologists is the widespread appearance of organisms with hard parts. Shells, spines and sheaths, of course, leave telltale traces

that feeble and naked jellylike floaters and opaque worms can't. In addition to the microbial hordes that inhabited Precambrian environments, multicellular organisms lived here and there by making their own nutrients with the help of solar or chemical energy or by scavenging for food in mud and among the remains of dead things. Predators that stalked and ate living creatures just didn't exist in large numbers. Much of early life was seemingly committed to garbage collecting.

In one scenario, scientists have suggested that the absence of predators in Precambrian times may have been due to low levels of free oxygen. Without good quantities of this gaseous elixir, Precambrian denizens would have had lower metabolic rates than their modern counterparts. As oxygen levels reached ten percent of modern concentrations at the dawn of the Palaeozoic Era, oxygen breathers got an unexpected boost. And with more activity probably came greater hunger pains. At some point, lowly sea creatures probably took a liking to live worm flesh and thereby innocently started a wild and exploratory revolution in body designs. The new and predatory behaviour sent an elementary but direct message to fellow creatures—defend yourself or be eaten.

The Palaeozoic movement for predation and self-defence was highly inventive. Different groups of animals employed a variety of chemical substances to create their hard parts. They included chiton (a flexible fingernail-like substance), calcium carbonate (limestone), silica (a glasslike material) and even a shield of sand that was glued onto the animal by a calcareous or silica cement.

The resulting arms race may explain why so many Cambrian creatures adopted different kinds of hard parts. Tubes, shields, claws, spines and shells not only created formidable weapons and defences but also gave their hosts a big advantage over soft-bodied competitors in almost all aspects of life. Hard parts were ultimately employed for less bloody endeavours by attaching muscles and tissue to help with locomotion or feeding. Trilobites, perhaps the world's most famous fossilized creatures, used segmented appendages for both scurrying across the ocean floor and trapping food. Given such specialization, all kinds of weird-looking creatures "exploded" onto the evolutionary scene, preparing Cambrian oceans for the world's first modern-looking ecosystems.

The appearance of hard parts in Palaeozoic organisms has also made it easier for scientists

Alberta's Rocky Mountains hold an abundance of early Palaeozoic rock.

to classify creatures on the basis of body architecture. Modern science recognizes approximately thirty living animal phyla. But fossils from the Burgess Shale and a southern Chinese quarry now hint that possibly another ten different phyla inhabited Palaeozoic seas, which expands the known diversity in animal designs by perhaps as much as thirty percent.

Many of the organisms that made Cambrian seas a teeming bouillabaisse have easily recognizable descendants (and make repeated appearances throughout this book). Porifera, or simple multicellular animals, are better known as sponges. They populated Cambrian seas in modest numbers. Their needlelike spines are the only hard parts that remain after death.

Coelenterates, whose current representatives include jellyfish, sea anemones and corals, existed in Precambrian waters. These ancient creatures typically possessed a primitive nervous system and well-developed muscle tissue. Some members such as coral didn't develop hard parts until the Ordovician Period. But

ever since then, they have played an important role in building ocean reefs.

Annelids, whose descendants include earthworms and leeches, burrowed in the mud of late Precambrian oceans. Until the arms race, these wormlike creatures left only ghostlike trails behind. But when they developed spines, hooklike appendages and jawlike mouths, their prehistoric crawlings became easier to decipher.

Brachiopods, creatures that look like clams, perhaps outnumbered all other life in shallow Cambrian seas. They attached themselves to the sea floor with a single stalklike pedicel. Although much less common today, these calcite-shelled creatures still live in oceans from pole to pole.

In contrast to the brachiopods, molluscs, with nearly a hundred thousand species, remain incredibly numerous. This famous clan includes the likes of snails, slugs, oysters, mussels and octopuses as well as many extinct members. By the middle of the Cambrian Period, snails and clams were present but not abundant.

Arthropods make up eighty percent of all visible creatures. Distinguished by an external skeleton and jointed legs and bodies, this phylum has a fantastically broad membership including shrimp, crabs, beetles, ants and lobsters. Trilobites were the most celebrated and abundant representatives during the Palaeozoic.

Echinoderms, such as starfish and sea urchins, exhibit a beautiful fivefold symmetry. The earliest echinoderms lived as scavengers or filter feeders. Later descendants include crinoids, or sea lilies.

Last but not least come the chordates, or all those creatures with a backbone. Fish, amphibians, reptiles, mammals and even modern Albertans belong to this group. During the Cambrian explosion, chordates possessed segmented muscles, a tail fin and a simple undivided notochord, or flexible backbone.

Other creatures that populated Cambrian seas disappeared as failed evolutionary experi-

ments or survive to this day in limited numbers. They include archaeocyathids (extinct cone-shaped bottom feeders), stromatoporoids (cabbage-shaped invertebrates), lacelike bryozoans, and graptolites (extinct creatures that occupied a twilight zone between invertebrates and chordates).

No fossil record better displays and details this glorious Cambrian world than the Burgess Shale. This world-famous mother lode of fossils was deposited in the soft muds and silts on the seaward side of an underwater reef. It probably loomed over the muddy sea floor as high as two hundred metres. Occasional storms churned the sea and likely cast animals and sediment over the reef's edge onto the sea floor, entombing the bottom dwellers. This explains why Burgess fossils contain a mixture of creatures that lived in warm shallow waters on top of the reef and in the dark cool depths of the

muddy sea floor. The creatures owe the fine preservation of their soft tissue to a fortuitous combination of factors—being entombed in sediment with low levels of oxygen in deep water.

More than 120 different species of animals and algal plants have been identified in the Burgess Shale. They include familiar Cambrian fare such as trilobites, sponges and brachiopods as well as a wealth of previously unknown creatures such as the fifty-centimetre-long *Anomalocaris*. This fearsome predator, which resembled a cuttlefish, possessed daggerlike spines arranged along two curved clawlike appendages that flanked its mouth. Since Walcott made his discovery, some scientists have claimed that there may be as many as ten separate phyla of creatures in the shale that bear little relationship to any other known animals, modern or ancient. Intense study is now under way to test this idea.

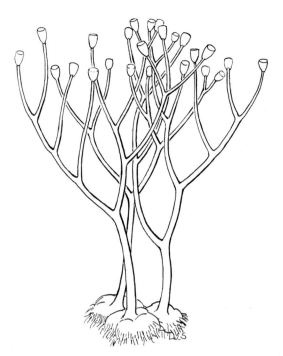

Cooksonia, a green pioneer with neither leaves nor roots, was among the very first plants to colonize the earth's land environment.

These unique and eccentric orphans come with otherworldly body shapes. *Wiwaxia,* a haunting oddball of an animal, which looks like a small plated pineapple with spines, probably crawled across the sea floor eating detritus. *Hallucigenia,* a tubelike beast, may have walked on seven pairs of tentacles and had two rows of unjointed spines along its back. Also present in this collection was the eel-like *Pikaia,* a member of the chordate group from which all creatures with backbones have descended, including humans.

The marked variation in body designs that characterize the Burgess fossils has deeply impressed palaeontologists. The variation indicates that perhaps for a brief time following the introduction of hard parts, the world was a rich place in which creatures with many different shapes and designs flourished. By the end of the Cambrian Period, the animal world lost diversity in design while slowly gaining variety among the few remaining anatomical models. Chance or simple luck, as opposed to bad design, may have sent *Wiwaxia* to oblivion and preserved our long-distant ancestor *Pikaia.* Notes Conway Morris, a palaeobiologist and longtime student of the Burgess Shale, "Imagine you were a time traveller and

you had no memory at all and were wandering around in the Cambrian world. Suppose someone came up to you and said, 'By the way, which species will radiate to produce other species and which will become extinct?' It seems as if there isn't any way in which one could predict."

The Green Revolution

Following the advent of hard parts and the deposition of the Burgess Shale, another story of geological importance took root along the world's shorelines. Here, marine plants began their historic migration to land, paving the way not only for a green planet but for all future dryland settlers.

Moving to the land was not an easy evolutionary adjustment for members of the plant kingdom because ocean living poses few worries. For starters, any part of their anatomy can draw in nutrients from seawater. As well, they do not need special structural support to remain upright in liquid. They also don't have to worry about water escaping from their tissues. The migration to land, however, meant that plants had to overcome such major obstacles as gathering food, supporting the body and preventing dehydration. But it was a vacant niche, and plants that could exploit it faced little competition.

Palaeobotanists don't know what the land first plant actually looked like or even where it first spread its greenery. But it may have been a type of algae or mosslike plant that formed a scum on exposed rocks along the shorelines of the Ordovician or Cambrian oceans. The oldest known vascular land plant fossil (415 million years old) belongs to late Silurian Europe. *Cooksonia,* which stood only a few centimetres tall, consisted of simple stalks that ended with spore-filled sacs. This green pioneer had neither leaves nor roots. By the end of the Silurian, plants only slightly more sophisticated than *Cooksonia* waved their sporey heads in ancient breezes around the world.

The Vertebrate Revolution

About the same time plants started their green conquest of the earth, fish, the first true vertebrates, made similar gains in Ordovician waters. Fossils in sedimentary rocks in Bolivia and Australia, as well as fossil scraps in the Harding Sandstone in Wyoming, document the appearance of animals with a backbone and internal skeleton about 470 million years ago. The first fish, some forty centimetres in length, possessed only a tail fin and looked like a small flexible torpedo with a head shield and scales. Scientists call them agnathans because they had no jaws and had to filter food through mouth and gill openings.

Throughout the remainder of the Ordovician and Silurian periods, jawless fish prospered as bottom feeders and possibly parasites in warm coastal waters. But at the end of the early Palaeozoic, about 410 million years ago, a new kind of fish possessing jaws constructed from modified gill bones prowled the seas. Fish with jaws doomed their agnathan cousins and inherited the oceans. The prowess of the jawed guaranteed that they would serve as the evolutionary source of all land vertebrates to come.

Although jawless fish probably plied Alberta's Palaeozoic seas, rocks have not yielded their fossilized remains. Agnathans, however, have been found in La Malbie, Quebec, Dease River, British Columbia, and in the Mackenzie Mountains of the Northwest Territories.

By late Ordovician and Silurian times, shallow seas had invaded North America from both the west and east. Few rocks in Alberta speak clearly of this age, but geologists speculate that the region once again became a tropical sea floor of limey muds, shoals and reefs for twenty million years. At the close of the Silurian Period, the seas were in retreat like an army weary of progressive marches. Another collision with Greenland and Europe encouraged the sea's departure by warping and uplifting the northern margin of North America.

And then a new era began with a cacophonic symphony that blasted the earth with music from emerging mountains, active volcanoes and cooking hydrocarbons.

Looking like a flexible torpedo, *Athenaegis* was a Silurian agnathan fish. A fossil of one was recently unearthed by Alberta palaeontologists working in the Northwest Territories.

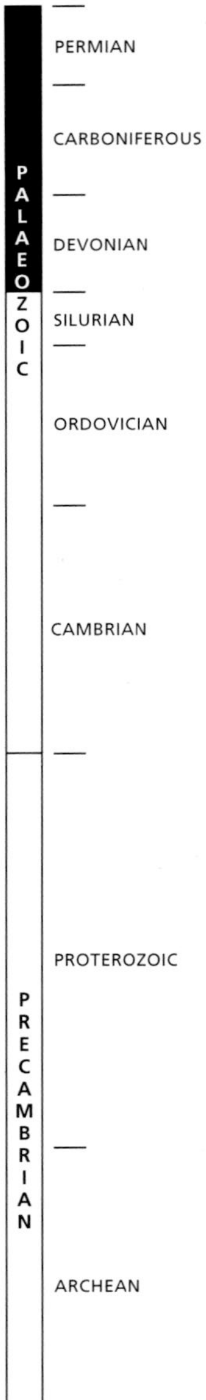

PERMIAN

CARBONIFEROUS

P
A
L
A
E
O
Z
O
I
C

DEVONIAN

SILURIAN

ORDOVICIAN

CAMBRIAN

PROTEROZOIC

P
R
E
C
A
M
B
R
I
A
N

ARCHEAN

HADEAN

32

Chapter Three

The Late Palaeozoic

Shaped like an ice-cream cone, rugose corals established crowded colonies along Alberta's great Devonian reefs.

The Devonian Developers

At Cirrus Mountain in the northeast corner of Banff National Park, a spectacular cliff looms over Highway 93. Known as the Weeping Wall, it is composed of drab grey Devonian and Carboniferous limestones with natural cavities. Upon closer inspection, the rock reveals the skeletal remains of a Devonian reef: fossilized coral, calcareous algae, stromatoporoids and other creatures. Among this cast of reef builders, stromatoporoids were the most abundant and important. They aren't a household name in Alberta, but given the scope and power of Alberta's oil industry, humble stromatoporoids should be.

Stromatoporoids—bulbous, calcareous spongelike creatures—constructed reefs across Devonian Alberta as formidable as the Great Barrier Reef of Australia. Their labours eventually covered hundreds of square kilometres, and some watery developments grew as high as a ten-storey building.

At the time, stromatoporoids didn't realize that they had conveniently established porous

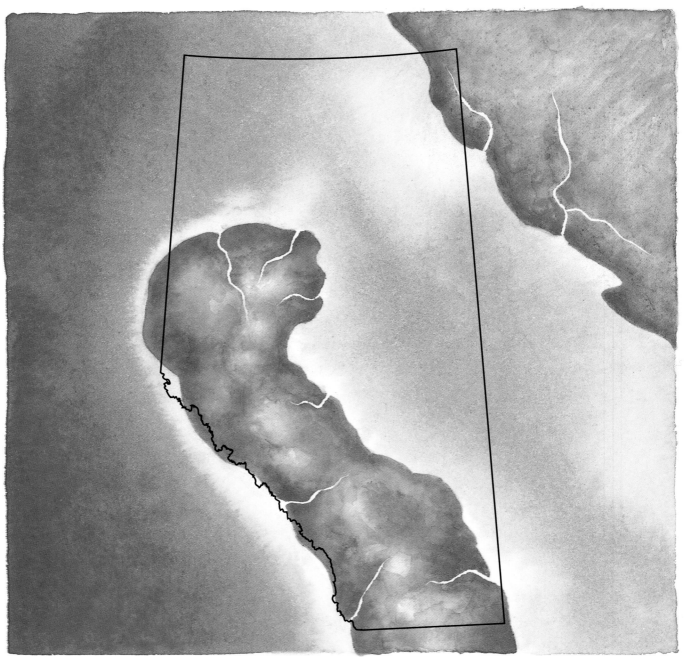

By the middle Devonian a peninsula the size of Florida stretched up from Montana, forcing the sea to enter Alberta from the north.

and permeable reservoirs for sixty percent of Alberta's future oil and gas reserves. But the oil-men who drilled nearly ten kilometres beneath the earth's surface at Leduc in 1947 were quick to recognize that their good fortune, western Canada's first great strike, owed much to the long labours of enigmatic stromatoporoids. For this reason, geologists refer to fossil stromato-poroids as Alberta's billion-dollar rock.

Just like modern reefs, Alberta's Palaeozoic structures offered shelter and food for myriad plants and animals. Delicate sea lilies anchored themselves to the reef in protected areas while clamlike brachiopods and ice-cream-cone-shaped rugose corals established crowded colonies all along the reef. In the shadows, sharks and large armoured placoderm fish chased smaller fish. *Dunkleosteus,* one of the largest of these predators, had a jaw gape a person could crawl into.

The growth of the great reefs slowly began in the middle of the Devonian Period. Ten to twenty million years prior to that time, Alberta had been high and dry. But then the Pacific Ocean gave the province a sus-tained bath. Blocked by the Western Alberta

Arch, a low north-projecting peninsula that extended from Montana to Peace River, the sea inched its way in from the north. Punctuated by long hundred-thousand-year retreats, the flooding progressed methodically, moving south through land made hilly by continental collisions. Whenever the seas retreated, huge pools of salt water larger than Great Salt Lake in Utah lay trapped in basins behind low ridges and reefs.

In the equatorially hot and dry climate of the Devonian, the water in these salt pools

The typical inhabitants of Alberta's Devonian reefs (above) included patrolling sharks, brachiopods and trilobites as well as sea lilies (below left) and solitary rugose corals (below middle and right).

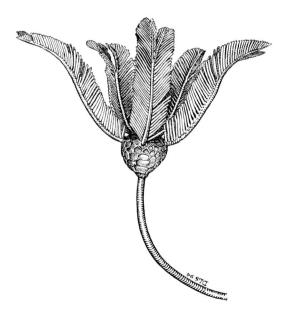

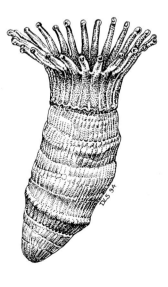

Late Palaeozoic rocks occur in the Northeast and in the Rockies.

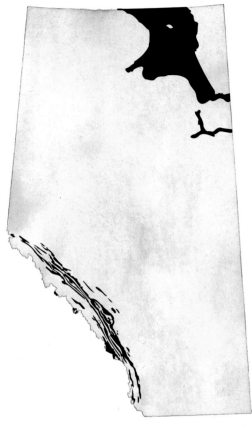

evaporated faster than the rains could replenish it. Over time, flooding and reflooding shifted these salt pans farther and farther south where they now form an integral part of western Canada's potash industry.

The sea's great push southward into Montana eventually eroded the Western Alberta Arch until it remained no more than an island separated from the southern and eastern mainland by more than six hundred kilometres of water. By the end of the Devonian, even this piece of land had been reclaimed by the Pacific.

In the shallow blue-green seas surrounding the flooded Arch and eastern mainland, a complex variety of reefs and banks made of the calcareous skeletons of dead marine creatures stretched forth like long bony fingers. The reefs extended irregularly from the Arch toward the north and east into central Alberta. Over tens of millions of years, as the shorelines shifted and water depths changed, new reef complexes formed while old ones drowned or were exposed to desert winds. By the close

of the Devonian Period, stromatoporoids and their reefal neighbours had fashioned a vast network of fossil and living reefs, buried or exposed, throughout Alberta.

But billion-dollar rocks alone do not account for Alberta's richness in oil and gas. To make these hydrocarbons takes a lucky combination of circumstances that really amounts to a long geological three-step recipe. The first and most important ingredient is a good supply of source rock rich in organic material such as the dead remains of marine plankton. The continued flooding of Alberta by Pacific waters amply furnished this Devonian ingredient by creating thick beds of organic ooze.

Then a good batch of bacteria must be added to the mixture. Their biological job is to remove most of the oxygen and nitrogen from the ooze, leaving behind mainly hydrogen and carbon. Cooking finally begins after millions of years when the heat and pressure of deep burial begins to transform the dead matter into liquid. The cooking must be precise, neither too hot (deep burial) nor too cold (shallow burial). In Alberta, just the right kind of cooking took place during the Mesozoic and Cenozoic eras as the land sagged under the weight of advancing slabs of rock that would eventually become the Canadian Rocky Mountains.

Last but not least, the oil must move out of the source rock into a natural underground reservoir. Stromatoporoids, of course, constructed the reefs so necessary for the collection of hydrocarbons. Although the workings of Devonian forces set the stage for the development of Alberta's oil, another 350 million years would pass before humans would discover what time and circumstance had hidden below Turner Valley, Leduc and Swan Hills.

The Devonian rocks that house much of Alberta's economic wealth lie not only kilometres below the prairie but kilometres above it in towering and jagged peaks. From the Crowsnest Pass northwest to Grande Cache,

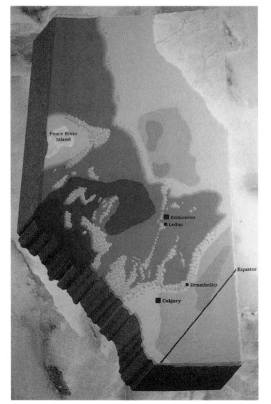

Devonian rock speaks of ancient seas and reefs. Highways 3, 1, 11 and 16 all pass through excellent expanses of such rock. Perhaps the most accessible and most dramatic limestone exposure lies on the north side of Lac Des Arcs outside of Canmore where the LaFarge concrete factory has cut off great slabs of Devonian limestone to make cement.

Beautiful displays of lower Carboniferous-aged rock, the so-called Banff and Rundle formations, make up the jagged peaks of Grotto and Pigeon Mountains, Mt. Lougheed, Mt. Norquay, Cascade Mountain and Mt. Rundle towering above the Banff townsite. In contrast, the sandstones, silts and shales of the Permian are more difficult to find in Alberta's fickle rock record. But rock aficionados can peek at this age in the Johnston and Ranger Canyon formations exposed along the Bow River near the Banff Springs Hotel.

Spectacular Devonian shales and limestones (above) mark the entrance to Jasper National Park.

Devonian Alberta (left): A geography in which great reefs (shown in green) stretched across a tropical sea.

With its Carboniferous limestones and shales, Mt. Rundle (above) looms over the townsite of Banff.

Primitive trees such as *Lepidodendron* (below) appeared in the late Palaeozoic.

The Birth of Pangea

As stromatoporoids and organic oozes laid the foundation for Alberta's economic wealth, continental plates continued their waltz in a stately reshaping of the configuration of the planet. During the early Devonian, Greenland and eastern Canada collided with northern Europe. This meeting gradually produced a mountain chain stretching from the northern tip of Greenland to Nova Scotia. Several million years later, a small plate consisting of parts of Siberia began to collide with the northern margin of North America, creating a mountain chain running east-west across what is now the Canadian Arctic. Tens of millions of years later, the collision of the western margin of North America with the Pacific Plate created a curved chain of volcanic islands hundreds of kilometres from the western shoreline. These island arcs looked much like Japan and the Philippines do today. In response to the sinking of the Pacific Plate, a deep trench formed between the arcs and the mainland.

The eternal tectonic waltz threw several continents into a collision with ancestral North America in the East and North. As continents joined in slow motion, they eventually formed a single landmass, which is now referred to as Laurasia. To the South, Africa, Antarctica, India and South America welded together to become Gondwana. By the end of the Permian, Gondwana and Laurasia had come together like a jigsaw puzzle to create a single global entity—Pangea.

As the continental plates converged, lands noisily warped, buckled and ripped. Some landmasses sank to become flooded while others heaved above the seas as new beach fronts for pioneering plants and insects. Where Europe and northern Asia collided, the mighty Urals rose. The Appalachians owe their existence to the collision of northwest Africa, southern Europe and southeast North America. The Adirondacks were also the product of the bumping and grinding that created Laurasia and Gondwana during the Devonian and Carboniferous periods. In the process, North America rotated clockwise and sluggishly moved twenty degrees north of the equator, bringing cooler weather that, in turn, began to kill off Alberta's great reefs.

While ancient Alberta experienced periodic flooding and reef building, plants were evolving throughout Laurasia and Gondwana. Building upon the simple structure of *Cooksonia,* green settlers developed leaves, roots and seeds. Soon ferns, scouring rushes and tree-sized plants dotted many landscapes. By the beginning of the Carboniferous Period, swamps, forests and grassless shrubby plains decorated the two supercontinents.

Into these new green environments insects advanced, followed eventually by crawling amphibians. Amphibians trace their ancestry to rhipidistians. Over a span of twenty million years this special group of fish with lungs and gills developed a revolutionary adaptation: limbs.

Capable of now stabilizing themselves in fast-moving rivers, the fish-turned-amphibians ventured awkwardly and briefly onto land. So began the age of four-footed creatures, or tetrapods.

Carboniferous and Permian Reptiles

During the first forty million years of the Carboniferous Period, amphibians tested life on land but never strayed too far from freshwater, which still sustained their eggs and hatchling larvae. However, a small group of creatures, cotylosaurs, gradually found new ways to sever their ties to rivers and ponds. From the cotylosaurs, an evolutionary intermediate between amphibians and reptiles, emerged the first true reptiles. These creatures were distinguished by

During the late Palaeozoic, the continents came together to form one global landmass, Pangea (above).

A Carboniferous coal swamp from the late Palaeozoic (below) was home to amphibians and giant dragonflies.

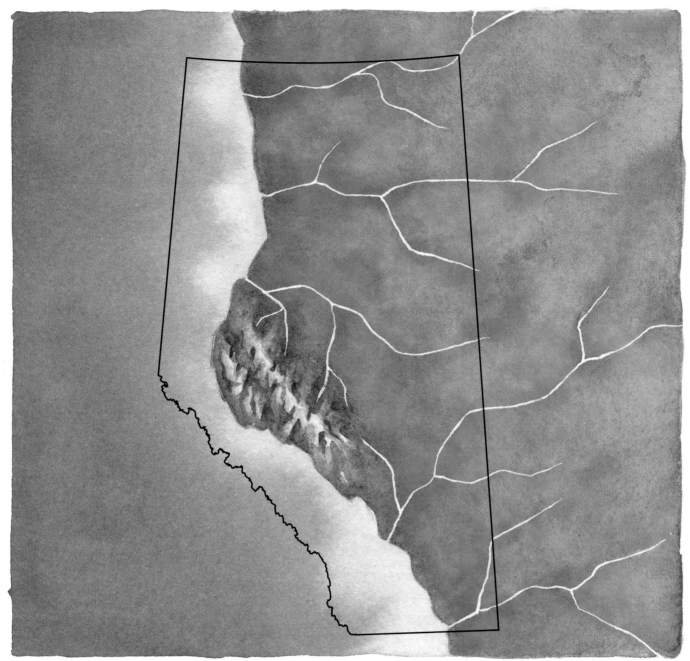

Permian Alberta: The land once again faced the mighty Pacific Ocean as shorelines advanced and retreated across the edge of North America.

their small size, agile limbs and the amniote egg. With its large shell and protective membranes, the amniote egg gave reptiles the freedom to lay their eggs on land.

The first reptiles to appear in the fossil record occur in Carboniferous tree trunks preserved in stone near Joggins, Nova Scotia. These small and compact creatures looked very much like modern lizards. But freed from their aquatic heritage, these reptiles diversified, colonizing different landscapes from their amphibian ancestors. Their descendants include all other reptiles, dinosaurs, birds and mammals. By the end of the

Permian, reptiles had begun to slink and crawl about in an amazing variety of forms. Two- to three-metre-long dimetrodons, for instance, prowled the equatorial plains of Pangea, using their telltale fan-shaped sails to regulate their body temperature. Meanwhile, mesosaurs, or small marine reptiles, explored shallow pools.

Carboniferous and Permian Landscapes

Scientists don't really know who ate whom in Palaeozic Alberta because not much evidence of land environments has been preserved. One interesting exception is found in the

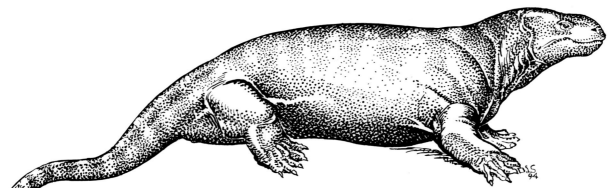

ancient river plain deposits that make up the Yahatinda Formation on the east face of Wapiti Mountain near Sundre. It consists of sandstones, siltstones and limestone conglomerates set down in and beside large river channels that flowed west across the Western Alberta Arch into the Pacific. From these ancient river deposits, geologists have collected broken fragments of jawless bottom-feeding fish and reedlike plants.

Farther north, along the border between Alberta and British Columbia, Carboniferous shales have yielded pieces of a scaly tree trunk, *Lepidodendron,* a swamp-loving plant that grew up to thirty metres in height. From this scanty evidence, geologists conclude that the land in late Palaeozoic Alberta had become home to an assortment of brave new plants and animals.

By the end of the Palaeozoic, as Pangea continued to form, life had achieved a kaleidoscope of forms in a growing richness of landscapes and seascapes. From the equator to the poles, the planet's climates and environments lost their cosmopolitan character and became more and more distinct. While deserts claimed the equator, swamps and forests covered the middle and high latitudes and glacial ice sheets silenced the land in the southern hemisphere. Plants and animals, of course, exploited these new living spaces with characteristic vigour.

In Panthalassa, the supersea that surrounded Pangea, thousands of species of worms, arthropods, brachiopods, clams and snails lived on the sea floor. Corals, bryozoans and crinoids, anchored to the seabed, occupied niches just above them. Plankton and free-swimming straight-shelled nautiloids, coiled ammonoids, plated fish and tiny mesosaurs swam above. On land, hundreds of kinds of tetrapods slunk about coniferous forests and plains interspersed with vast deserts and snow-capped mountains. Mammal-like reptiles now ruled the terrestrial world. This bountiful celebration of life, however, did not last long.

A sampling of cotylosaurs, an evolutionary intermediate between amphibians and reptiles: *Diadectes* (above), *Limnoscelis* (middle) and *Seymouria* (below).

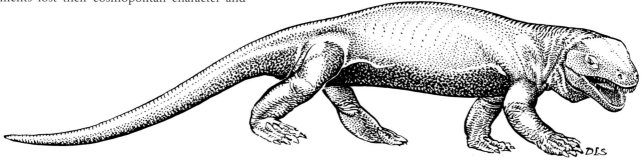

On the banks of a Permian river (above), a *Dimetrodon* defends dinner, the carcass of a *Diadectes*.

Mesosaurus (below), a small swimming reptile, ate mostly fish.

The Great Dying

The Permian extinction stands as a singular event in the planet's history. During less than one million years, ninety-five percent of all Earth species vanished. In contrast, the infamous dying that claimed all the dinosaurs at the end of the Mesozoic Era culled only sixty-five percent of the world's species. The Permian killing, then, makes the great dinosaur demise look like a mere junior partner in extinction.

Scientists have long known about the Permian die-off. Eighteenth and nineteenth century fossil hunters regularly noted that life changed strikingly as the Palaeozoic ended and the Mesozoic began. The rocks testify that not much survived the Permian extinction. The sea, for example, lost many of its original inhabitants: trilobites, crinoids, ammonoids, several kinds of brachiopods and armoured fish. On land, the mammal-like reptiles were reduced to a handful of survivors.

The exact cause of so many extinctions over such a short time remains a mystery. Some scientists suggest that an asteroid may have hit the earth 250 million years ago, decimating sea and land life. But no evidence of such a catastrophe has been found. Other palaeontologists have proposed that falling sea levels at the end of the Palaeozoic reduced living space for marine creatures. The ensuing competition for food may have led to great marine die-offs, they argue. However, this scenario doesn't explain the land extinctions.

The so-called suffocation hypothesis is the most recent and interesting explanation. It suggests that many Permian communities were deprived of oxygen and essentially suffocated. According to this theory, the shrinking of the seas may have caused concentrations of the earth's atmospheric oxygen to decrease while carbon dioxide increased. As the seas fell over thousands of years, a natural oxidation or burning of organic material along the drying shorelines might have produced such calamitous atmospheric changes. If the oxygen supply fell to one-half its modern levels, which appears possible, then many terrestrial creatures would have suffocated.

The ocean killings would have come next. As a result of a global greenhouse effect triggered by rising amounts of carbon dioxide, glaciers melted and seas rose at the end of the Palaeozoic. As is typical of such dramatic rises in sea levels, many areas of the ocean floor became oxygen starved.

So a few hundred thousand years after the land die-offs, marine communities, too, may have smothered. However plausible this theory may be, it still does not explain why some groups of creatures died and others survived.

Fossils, it seems, do not yield all the secrets of vanished kingdoms.

By the end of the Palaeozoic
Era, primitive reptiles like
Petrolacosaurus (above) had
branched out into several
groups of creatures such
as the lumbering herbivore
Scutosaurus (middle), and
the deadly predator,
Dimetrodon (below).

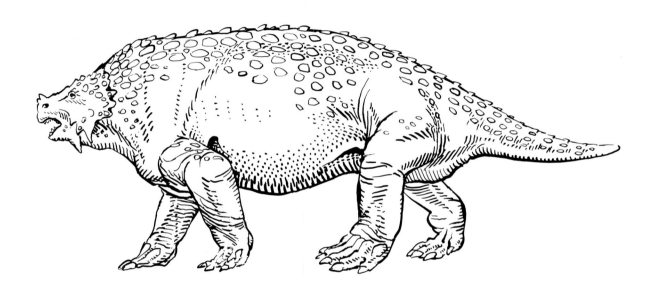

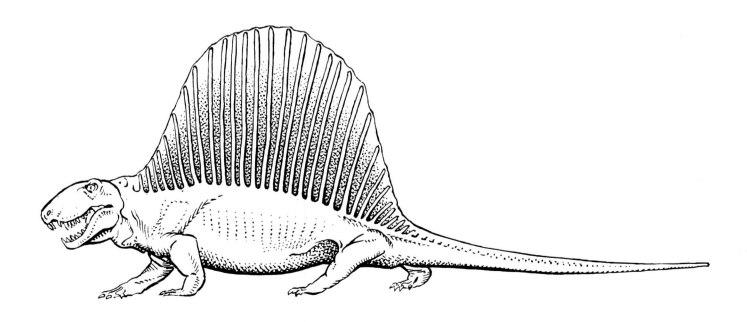

MESOZOIC

JURASSIC

TRIASSIC

PERMIAN

CARBONIFEROUS

DEVONIAN

SILURIAN

PALAEOZOIC

ORDOVICIAN

CAMBRIAN

PROTEROZOIC

PRECAMBRIAN

ARCHEAN

HADEAN

BUDGEN

Chapter Four

The Early Mesozoic

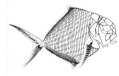

Mesozoic mariners: *Albertonia* (above) and *Bobasatrania* (below) both navigated Alberta's ancient coastline.

For the last forty years, Canadian geologists and palaeontologists have trekked by foot, float-plane and packhorse to a frigid glacial lake midway between Grande Prairie, Alberta, and Prince George, British Columbia. To the scientists, the trip is not only a high Rocky Mountain adventure but a voyage back into time, some 225 million years ago. Their destination, Wapiti Lake and its wild surroundings, offers intrepid visitors a vast treasure of fossils encased in rock.

The many fish and reptile specimens recovered by Royal Tyrrell Museum palaeontologists indicate that a variety of creatures lived off Alberta's ancient west coast during the early Mesozoic Era. Divided into three periods (Triassic, Jurassic and Cretaceous), the Mesozoic—the era of "middle life"—was once thought to be a time when many plants and animals straddled the borders of primitive life and a better world. But the creatures of the Mesozoic were neither half-primitive nor half-modern; they were simply well suited to the land and waters of their time.

The Wapiti Lake fossils speak of intriguing

From fossil-rich shales near Wapiti Lake (above), palaeontologists have recovered the remains of ichthyosaurs such as *Pessosaurus* (below), the fiercest marine reptiles that ever lived.

Triassic adaptations to marine environments. Of the more than twenty different kinds of fish recovered from the site, perhaps the strangest were *Albertonia* and *Bobasatrania*. They both navigated Alberta's coastline, which then stretched from Hay River to Lethbridge. *Albertonia* looked like a regular fish, about half a metre long, but possessed absurdly long pectoral fins. These appendages may have come in handy for short bursts of speed, stirring up food from the ocean floor or even heated sexual displays.

In contrast, *Bobasatrania* looked like an oddball and possessed a giant diamond-shaped pancake body. Poorly developed teeth on its jaw and a well-developed battery of teeth along its throat suggest a diet of shrimp and small fish. Sharks, barracudalike predators and other more familiar-looking fish kept *Albertonia* and *Bobasatrania* company.

The Wapiti Lake fossils record another important Triassic occurrence: the invasion of seawaters by reptiles. After the great Permian dying, four unrelated groups of reptiles colonized the earth's great ocean, Panthalassa. They included ichthyosaurs (dolphin-shaped reptiles), nothosaurs (so-called fake lizards with long necks and paddlelike flippers), thalattosaurs (the reptilian equivalent of a sea otter) and placodonts (mollusc-eaters).

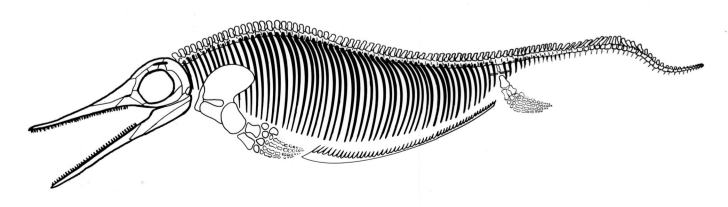

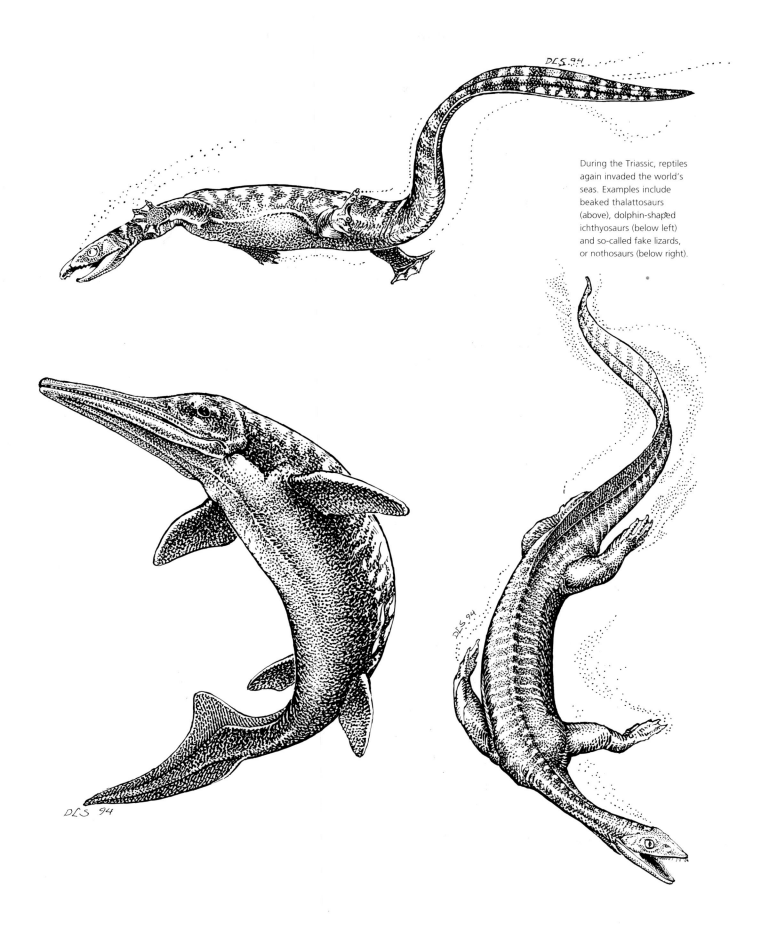

During the Triassic, reptiles again invaded the world's seas. Examples include beaked thalattosaurs (above), dolphin-shaped ichthyosaurs (below left) and so-called fake lizards, or nothosaurs (below right).

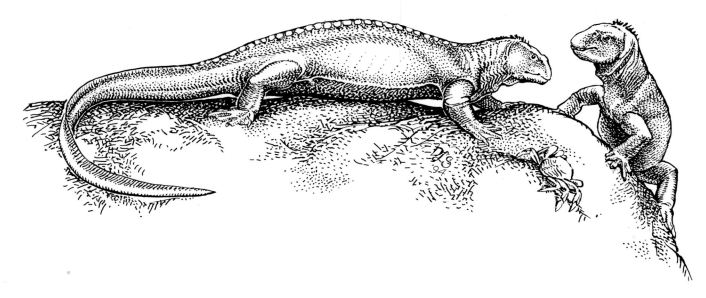

Equipped with robust teeth, placodonts (above) munched on a diet of snails and clams.

Cycads, such as *Leptocycas* (below left), as well as ferns greened Mesozoic lands. The Rockies ably display rocks of this period (below right).

According to Wapiti Lake's fossil record, the earth's earliest and fiercest marine reptiles lived and died by the continent's coast. *Utatsusaurus* and *Grippia,* for example, are among the oldest and most primitive known ichthyosaurs in the world. Their snakelike bodies, crushing teeth and weak paddles give palaeontologists a snapshot of ichthyosaur origins. More advanced ichthyosaurs, such as the dolphin-shaped fisheaters *Mixosaurus* and *Pessosaurus,* hunted in the same waters millions of years later.

Perhaps the most unusual fossil reptile collected from talus slopes around Wapiti Lake is *Thalattosaurus.* At home on both land and sea, this sea-otter-like creature may have fed on jellyfish and basked on the beach under a Triassic sun.

But Wapiti Lake has also yielded other Mesozoic surprises. In 1986, Dr. Donald Brinkman and his field party from the Royal Tyrrell Museum of Palaeontology discovered the skull of a peculiar reptile—*Wapitisaurus problematicus.* The creature appears to be related to a family of land-dwelling gliding reptiles, the coelurosauravids. The puzzle is this: what is the close relative of a land-loving creature doing in marine sediments? Either *Wapitisaurus* is a cousin of gliders that returned to the sea or a land creature whose carcass was given a watery burial. Until the

rest of the skeleton is found, the Triassic riddle of the true character of *Wapitisaurus* will remain just that—another riddle of the past.

The Rocky Mountains harbour other evidence of Triassic sea life. The fossils of small coiled ammonoids, a ubiquitous Mesozoic denizen related to squids, dot the Spray River Group and Fernie Formation in eastern British

Columbia. These grey rocks, which also contain heavily ribbed clams, speak, too, of changes in geography and climate. South of the village of Cadomin, outside of Jasper National Park, a sliver of Spray River Group rocks reminds Albertans of a time when siltstones and sandstones collected in deep cool waters. The next layer contains limestones formed in shallow warm-water ocean settings. And on top lie evaporated salts that accumulated as shorelines retreated into British Columbia, leaving hot and dry tidal flats along Alberta's west coast.

A careful observer will also find in this group testament of another sort: the pencil-shaped remains of belemnites scattered among black shale. During medieval times, people thought the belemnite's rod-shaped internal skeletons were the fingernails of devils. But palaeontologists have now identified the creatures as another relative of the ancient squid. Piles of belemnite remains ten or more deep in Spray River Group rock indicate mysterious mass dyings in Mesozoic seas.

Elsewhere in the world, the Triassic brought an enviable stability. Throughout Pangea, seasonal rains and monsoons came and went while great rivers patiently cut across plains to the coast where ocean brines slowly evaporated. A new group of reptiles, thecodonts, prowled some of these landscapes, picking their way through seed ferns, horsetails, cycads and cone-bearing conifers.

They possessed toothy skulls and long four-legged bodies, and looked like crocodiles. Thecodonts, the ancestors of true crocodiles and dinosaurs, inherited a land left empty by the mammal-like reptiles killed during the Permian dying. By the end of the Triassic, they also acquired a new food source—small, furry and ratlike creatures called mammals.

But in geological terms, all stable things generally come undone, and by the end of the Triassic, the forces of plate tectonics began to rip Pangea apart along the very seams that had once joined it together. Where the land ripped open, deep canyons or rifts formed, and from the opened earth, lava oozed to cover the floors of rift valleys. The ocean, forever eager to reclaim land, gradually turned the rifts into coastlines. When sea levels rose, the oceans submerged the continents of North

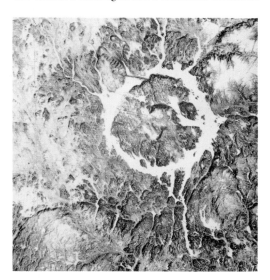

Coiled ammonites (above left) are a common Mesozoic signature in Alberta.

Wapitisaurus problematicus (above right) is a palaeontological conundrum.

Quebec's Manicouagan crater (below) serves as a raw reminder of the power of asteroid bombardments.

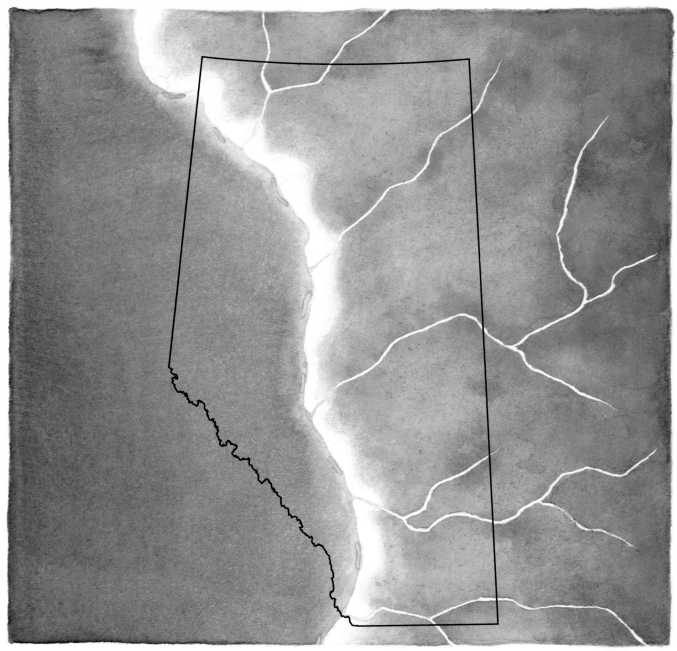

Triassic Alberta: A lush Pacific shoreline punctuated by wild rivers.

America, Eurasia, South America, Africa, India and Antarctica, turning them into mere collections of islands. By the end of the Jurassic, mighty Pangea was no more. The earth was a watery world dotted with island continents.

The Triassic's end came with several bangs as a clump of asteroids slammed into Earth. The impact of this space debris left prominent calling cards that include the giant Manicouagan crater in Quebec and grains of shocked quartz in three different layers of marine rock in Italy. Altered by high-velocity impact, the quartz grains suggest that at least

three separate asteroids, all part of a swarm, bombarded Earth. Geologists speculate that each collision may have been separated by many tens of thousands of years.

The extinctions, which may have followed the asteroid bombardments, and the resulting global chaos would have been dramatic. In the seas, snails, clams and ammonites suffered great losses, while nothosaurs, thalattosaurs and placodonts vanished altogether. On land, insects recorded heavy casualties while the thecodonts died out. Mammals survived the extinction but remained small and inconspic-

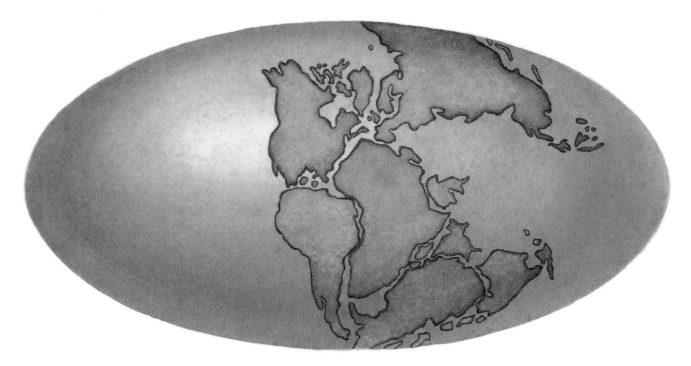

uous, seemingly unable to capitalize on the extinction of their thecodont predators. But two relatively small groups of creatures, dinosaurs and crocodiles, took advantage of the land vacated by the extinct thecodonts. The Age of Dinosaurs had begun.

Terrible Lizards

The word *dinosaur* has always meant different things to different people. In the mid-nineteenth century, a London surgeon and bone collector, Richard Owen, first invented the word, which means "terrible lizard," to describe fossilized reptile bones thought to belong to extinct and unbelievably large lizards. In this century, school children commonly describe dinosaurs as big monsters with even bigger appetites.

Palaeontologists, who pay a great deal of attention to classifying creatures, predictably offer a more elaborate definition. According to these scientists, the Dinosauria includes creatures that share a number of prominent skeletal features. Among the group, many scientists place an unlikely looking dinosaur descendant—the birds. To belong to this famous club, a creature must have long bones in the palate, three or more vertebrae where the hips attach to the backbone, a shoulder joint that faces backwards and an index finger with three or fewer joints. Although this technical definition of Dinosauria has been carefully developed over the last fifteen years, it is neither easy to remember nor visually distinctive.

Birds, of course, complicate the issue. As living descendants of meat-eating dinosaurs, these feathered denizens have all of the bony trademarks that set dinosaurs apart from other creatures. Yet, in popular culture, a dinosaur remains a terrible lizard without feathers.

Two hundred and ten million years ago, Pangea came undone, creating the Atlantic Ocean (above).

Thecodonts, such as *Chasmatosaurus* (below), were crocodilelike carnivores of the Triassic that slowly evolved into dinosaurs and true crocodiles.

During the Jurassic, the fanciful monsters that so fascinate children evolved like a fabulous cast of characters. *Allosaurus* (right), an early carnivore, and *Brachiosaurus* (below), a thirty-tonne vegetarian with a whiplike tail, were examples of Jurassic dinosaurs.

The classic or nonfeathered dinosaurs can be loosely defined in the following easy-to-remember way. They moved with their legs tucked under their bodies, unlike lizards and crocodiles, which prowled on legs sticking out of their sides. Dinosaurs walked on their toes just like modern birds. They lived only on land and did not swim or fly. (Reptilian swimmers and flyers go by other names such as mesosaurs and pterosaurs). In sum, dinosaurs were egg-laying reptiles that walked on their toes, kept their legs tucked under their bodies and lived on land only during the Mesozoic Era. All are now extinct.

Dinosaurs evolved from a stock of thecodont reptiles sometime during the middle of the Triassic. But palaeontologists are still trying to answer the question of why they evolved as they did. Ever since vertebrates first crawled onto the land in the late Palaeozoic, the process of natural selection has gradually improved the walking and running ability of four-legged creatures.

Throughout the Triassic (and long before), the legs of many animal groups underwent a number of modifications. For starters, they had been partially or completely brought up under the body, developing a straight up and down look. They had also become longer. During the Triassic, a variety of mammal-like reptiles and thecodonts experimented with muscle and bone, and developed legs that moved forward and backward rather than out to the side. The amphibian swagger now had competition.

In the midst of this experimentation, a new kind of walker appeared: the biped. Thecodonts were probably the first to run on their hind legs when chasing prey or evading predators. But some of the earliest dinosaurs, a group of highly specialized thecodonts, employed this novel means of getting about full time. Palaeontologists don't know if all early dinosaurs moved solely on their hind legs but most agree that dinosaurs were able walkers and runners, achieving speeds of more than ten kilometres per hour, with the quickest achieving speeds two to five times as fast. With their limbs strategically located under their bodies, ankle joints flexing front-to-back and legs made longer by virtue of walking on toes, the dinosaurs could outrun almost every other Mesozoic creature. These features, when combined with the advantage of having liberated the front limbs from walking, explain why dinosaurs filled the plains and jungles of disintegrating Pangea in the Triassic's twilight.

Although initially diminished by the mass extinctions at the end of the Triassic, the dinosaurs quickly recovered and soon became the undisputed masters of all life on land for the next 145 million years. During the Jurassic, all the fanciful monsters that so fascinate children evolved like a cast of characters from a science fiction book. Giant long-necked sauropods weighing up to ninety tonnes lived side-by-side with agile chicken-sized compsognathids. Predatory allosaurs, or mean-looking meateaters, tangled with stegosaurs and ankylosaurs—the armoured tanks of their day. Other popular dinosaurs such as tyrannosaurs, pack-hunting dromaeosaurs, long-necked bird-mimic dinosaurs, duck-billed hadrosaurs and sturdy ceratopsians didn't make

their thundering debut until the Cretaceous Period.

The long-term success of dinosaurs was indirectly related to other global happenings. The emergence of Tethys, a narrow seaway separating the northern and southern hemispheres, produced good dinosaur weather. Warm Tethyan waters flowing away from the equator helped to increase rainfall and create a tropical world from pole to pole. The seaway slowly replaced the deserts of the Triassic with rivers, lakes, swamps, coastal forests and giant inland seas—a dinosaur paradise.

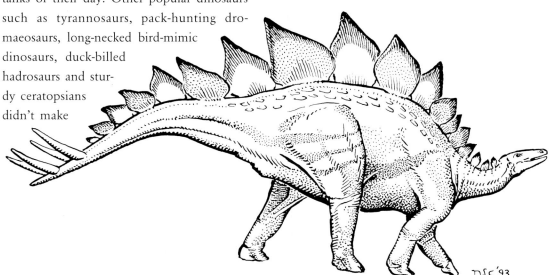

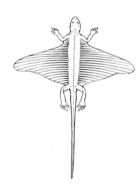

Modifications of body form for flight (above) have occurred in birds (top), pterosaurs (middle) and gliding reptiles (bottom).

Archaeopteryx, the oldest known bird (below), looked more like a dinosaur than its modern descendants.

Taking Flight

As dinosaurs shook up the early Mesozoic world, another group of strange backboned creatures took to the air. Although insects like dragonflies first properly evolved the wonders of powered flight in the late Palaeozoic, the only vertebrate to make a passable effort had been a gliding Permian reptile. Coelurosauravid reptiles had used grossly expanded ribs and skin as a novel airfoil. But the Triassic fossil record clearly gives the pterosaur, a close cousin to the dinosaurs, full credit for being the first backboned animal to use powered flight.

Pterosaur wings, which spanned anywhere from sixty centimetres to fifteen metres—the length of eight humans—consisted of an enormously long fourth finger, or strut, and a large sheet of leathery skin that stretched from the finger to the body. Hollow bones and a skin membrane from the hand to the neck provided additional stability. Pterosaurs, some of which may have fished like pelicans and been covered with fur, were enduring beasts. They survived the Triassic die-off and coexisted with their dinosaur cousins until the end of the Cretaceous.

The earliest known bird fossils come from limestone deposits in Solnhofen, Germany. There, among the shallow sea remains of ammonites, tree twigs and pterosaurs, scientists found a nearly complete and feathered skeleton of *Archaeopteryx* in 1861. The toothed jaw, bony tail, clawed fingers and feather imprint suggest a creature half-dinosaur and half-bird.

Unlike the kitelike appendages of pterosaurs, the wings of ancient and modern birds consist of a fused hand, feathers and skin. Feathers, which are actually highly modified scales, probably first appeared among a group of dinosaurs as a novel way to insulate the body.

Although *Archaeopteryx* flapped across Jurassic skies 140 million years ago, the first birds probably evolved much earlier. But given that birds descended from dinosaurs (their skeletal structures are nearly identical), it's unlikely scientists will be able to identify avian creatures older than *Archaeopteryx* unless feather imprints are found with them—an unlikely palaeontological proposition.

As dinosaurs began their epic conquest of the earth, life in Alberta continued to be hot and dry. By the middle of the Jurassic, as the global climate became wetter, forests and swamps sprouted along Alberta's coast. North America's slow drift to the northwest continued, taking the province to its present latitude far from the torrid heat of the tropics. As sea levels rose, the ocean washed over southern Alberta, Saskatchewan and Manitoba. This huge seaway, similar in size to the modern Gulf of Mexico, bathed the coast with warm water.

Prelude to the Rockies

But while seawater once again played with the land, volcanic island arcs off the coast began to collide with western North America. Volcanic arcs like those of the Japanese and Philippine archipelagoes usually signal great subterranean movements. Carried along on a conveyor belt of tectonic plates that slid under the North American crust, these arcs piled off the conveyor and slowly butted against the western margin of North America. Over millions of years, the rocks of the volcanic islands, tortured by intense pressure and heat, effectively glued themselves to the western margin of the continent.

These collisions had a dramatic impact on the western fringes of North America. Rock layers that had taken tens of millions of years to form were gradually pushed up from ancient sea floors, bent, broken and thrust to the east. Where these colossal forces weakened the earth's crust, large plumes of molten magma flowed toward the surface, baking surrounding rocks and turning into vast under-

ground oceans of solid granite. The jumbled remains of these island arcs, ancient sea floors and granite oceans can be seen throughout mountain ranges in eastern British Columbia, including the Ominecas, Cassiars, Cariboos, Selkirks, Skeenas and Purcells.

The great smashing of volcanic arcs against western Canada radically changed Alberta's geography. An outcrop of late Jurassic rock along the Trans-Canada Highway just east of the Banff exit ramp records one of the consequences—the final retreat of the Pacific Ocean. The Fernie Formation and Kootenay Group stand as momentous ocean exit signs and look like a giant stack of tipped-over plywood sheets.

The titans of geology—uplift and erosion—deposited the Fernie and Kootenay sediments over a twenty-million-year period in a narrow ocean basin that slowly disappeared as the island arcs pushed against western Canada. Like a zipper closing, the island arcs collided first in the south and then worked their way

northward. As geological forces zipped landmasses together, the last remnant of the Pacific Ocean spilled northward out of Alberta.

The Fernie Formation records this process and includes levels of deep-water marine shales and sands, and shallow-water shales. The Kootenay Group also includes beach sands and, for the first time in Alberta's history, a new kind of rock—coal.

The Age of Coal

Coal's appearance in Alberta tells a unique story about climatic change and sediment preservation. Like oil, the making of coal involves a precise and lengthy recipe. First, peat or thick layers of wet plant debris must build up in swamps or coastal wetlands where wet climates and soggy soil smile upon plant growth. Second, the peat must be buried in airtight environments so it does not dry out and burn. The repeated flooding of swamps and wetlands with stagnant water often acts as an effective seal.

The dramatic collision of volcanic island arcs against western Canada had rocky consequences such as the Skeena Mountains in western British Columbia.

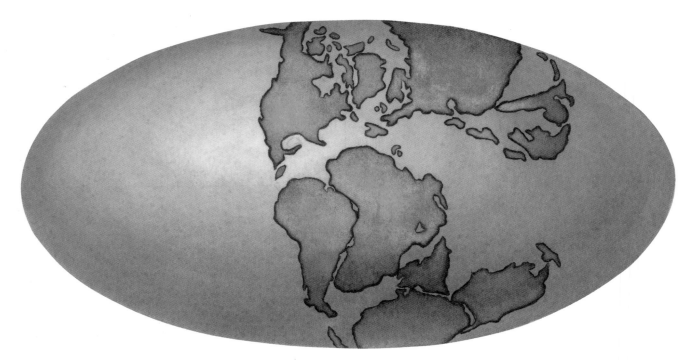

By the end of the Jurassic, the continents had assembled themselves into an easily recognizable configuration (above).

The Alberta basin, which contains oil, gas, coal and dinosaurs, was formed as stacked thrust sheets caused the earth's crust to sag (below).

About ten metres of wet peat are needed to create one metre of coal. Thus, to get the water depth needed for very thick peat beds to form, the land must either sink or water levels must rise. Then bacteria must partly decompose the peat before it is buried deeply enough to transform dead plants into coal. To accomplish this final act, the land must sink, allowing hundreds of metres of new sediment to pile on top. Last, if the coal is to be shovelled by miners' hands, then geological forces must raise the concoction from the deep closer to the surface.

At the end of the Jurassic, Alberta honoured most of these conditions with wet warm swamps along its coast. But most importantly it offered its peat a sinking basin. The basin was formed by heavy slabs of rock thrust up by island arc collisions. The great weight of these sheets depressed the earth's crust and caused it to sag between the thrust of the sheets on the west side and the more stable parts in eastern Alberta. Extending south from northern British Columbia to Montana, the Alberta basin was long and narrow. It gave the exiting Pacific Ocean a pathway and offered Jurassic sand, silt, mud and coal a convenient resting place. Sediments poured into this trap from the west, south and east as the newly formed mountains eroded. Under the weight of the rock sheets and new sediment, the basin continued to sink, burying peat swamps—the precursors to coal.

To ancient birds, the Alberta basin remained a prominent landmark until the end of the Tertiary Period, a span of a hundred million years. A stable and long-lived feature, it played a major role in shaping Alberta's geology. This remarkable peat-maker eventually shifted farther east into the province where it became a tomb not only for coal but for dinosaurs in the Cretaceous Period.

Alberta's powerful Jurassic legacy became a formidable fifty-year-long economic boom in the Crowsnest Pass at the turn of the century. A trip down Highway 3 into the old mining towns of Bellevue, Hillcrest and Frank gives travellers a glimpse of the black rock's power-

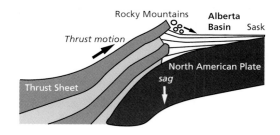

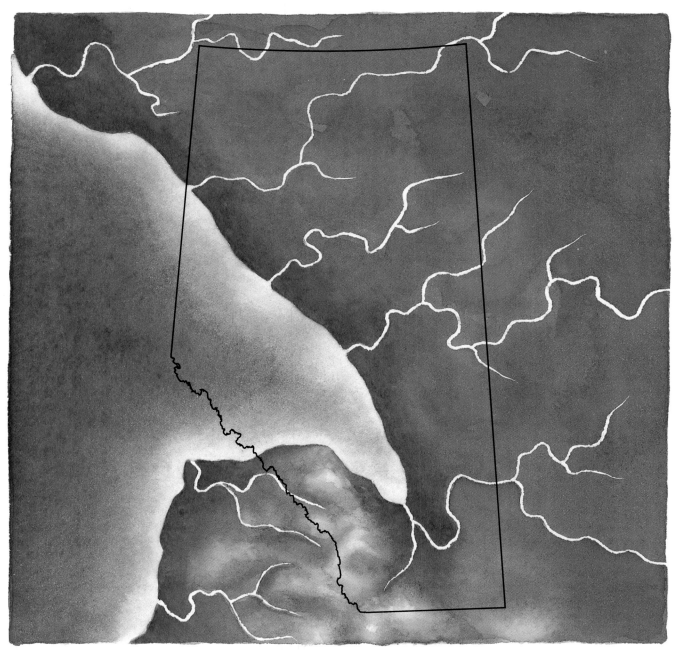

As island arcs closed in on Alberta at the end of the Jurassic the sea retreated north.

ful hold on the region. Here, the ambitions of European miners, union leaders and French and American business tycoons met uneasily over shiny semianthracite coal embedded deep in the mountains. In 1903, the notorious Frank Slide abruptly entombed seventy-three miners and obliterated much of the town of Frank with limestone boulders the size of houses. And in the 1930s, the neighbouring town of Blairmore witnessed some of Canada's bloodiest labour struggles. At the time, none of the Albertans involved recognized how their individual destinies had been irrevocably tied to Jurassic upheavals that happened more than 150 million years ago.

MESOZOIC
CRETACEOUS
JURASSIC
TRIASSIC

PALAEOZOIC
PERMIAN
CARBONIFEROUS
DEVONIAN
SILURIAN
ORDOVICIAN
CAMBRIAN

PRECAMBRIAN
PROTEROZOIC
ARCHEAN
HADEAN

Chapter Five

The Late Mesozoic

Joseph Burr Tyrrell, an explorer and adventurer, was the first white man to document coal and dinosaur graveyards in Alberta's badlands.

In the spring of 1884, the Geological Survey of Canada placed Joseph Burr Tyrrell, a twenty-six-year-old explorer from Weston, Ontario, in charge of an expedition to study the shape and age of a "veritable kingdom" of prairie north of the Bow River. As the young geologist travelled across the open and grassy plains with a party of three, he admittedly felt like a "young mariner who wishes to sail his ship within sight of shore rather than strike out across the boundless ocean."

When Tyrrell reached the muddy Red Deer River, he decided to paddle south in a folding canvas canoe into the badlands, Alberta's grand and awesome vista of the Cretaceous Period. Two days later at Kneehill Creek, Tyrrell found a good assortment of dinosaur bones. Farther down the river, he passed huge outcrops of coal at the future site of Drumheller.

Particularly intrigued by the bones, he returned again to Kneehill Creek in August only to discover the skull "of a large extinct reptile." At the time, one North American palaeontologist marvelled at the size of the

find, calling it "the largest dinosaur yet found in Laramie"—a comment referring to the late Cretaceous and early Cenozoic deposits associated with the uplift of the Rocky Mountains. When later prepared and classified, the sharp-toothed carnivore *Albertosaurus sarcophagus* was regarded as a three-quarter-size relative of *Tyrannosaurus rex*. Although Tyrrell later went on to explore the barren lands of the Canadian arctic tundra and make his fortune in the Kirkland Lake gold camp, the Cretaceous graveyard that he found eventually gained far greater fame than its discoverer. Today, the remarkable dinosaur bone fields of southern Alberta are matched in richness only by the vast prehistoric graveyards in China's Gobi Desert and parts of the United States.

Cretaceous Landscapes

The verdant estuaries and coastal bays that sheltered and nourished the herds of dinosaurs that once dominated Alberta gradually appeared as the result of several momentous

forces. The sinking and widening of the Alberta basin, the union of Arctic and southern seas and global climatic changes all helped to create a land that welcomed and beckoned an incredible diversity of dinosaurs from duck-billed hadrosaurs to flesh-eating tyrannosaurs.

The making of this mythical dinosaur land began as usual with geological collisions. During the Cretaceous and subsequent Cenozoic, more island arcs periodically bumped up against the western coast. Five collisions occurred, each lasting approximately ten million years, followed by a few million years of tectonic quiet. Each collision built upon the last slow-motion smashup and followed a telltale pattern with the uplifting, folding, breaking and thrusting of rock toward the east. In some cases, volcanic eruptions added sympathetic drama to the scene by spewing vast plumes of dust and ash into the prevailing winds from the west. In this manner, most of British Columbia was slowly cobbled onto western Canada.

But all this extra force had the effect of extending the reach of the Alberta basin from the present-day foothills well into Saskatchewan. Advancing sheets of rock and the subsequent sediment unleashed by erosion sank

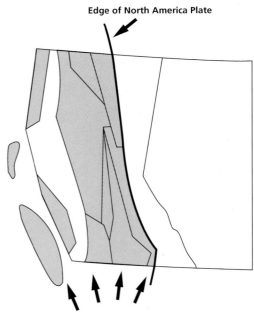

Edge of North America Plate

Island Arcs welded to North America

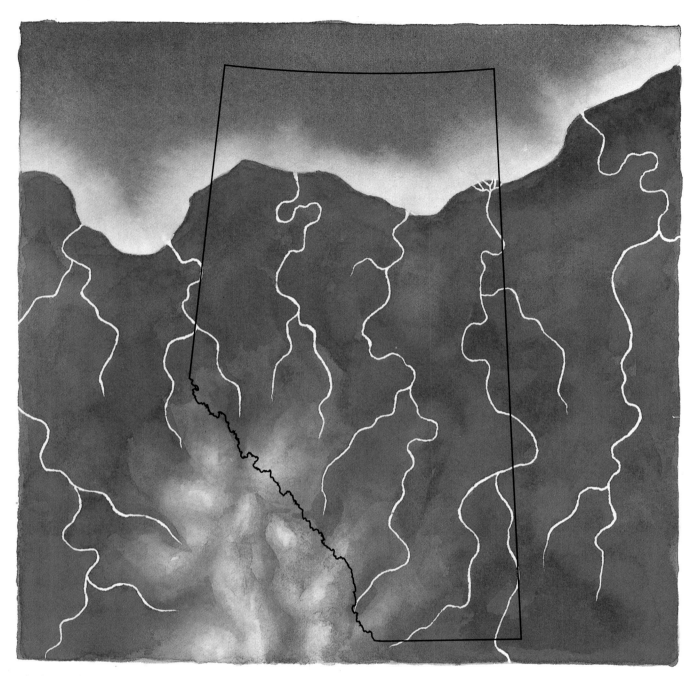

the basin deeper and deeper. With each new collision, the basin sagged, and as it sank, the Arctic sea swept into the province from the north. At the same time, vast amounts of mud and other debris poured in from the west as new mountains made of ancient sea floor and volcanic rock were lifted and exposed to geology's dependable helpers—wind, rain and cold. Over fifty million years, the western part of the Alberta basin filled with layers of marine and nonmarine sediment more than three kilometres thick.

Western Canada, however, wasn't the only landscape that was sinking and sagging. As the North American plate continued moving westward in the late Mesozoic, the entire west coast fell under the spell of collisions with island arcs. Through Montana, Wyoming, Colorado and farther south into New Mexico and Texas, the Western Interior of the continent sank in rerock piling up on the coast. As sea levels rose during the Cretaceous, arms of the Arctic Ocean and the Gulf of Mexico invaded these basins eventually meeting in

Early Cretaceous Alberta: The sea retreated to the north as muddy rivers poured into the sea from the west, south and east.

A volcano erupting nearly a hundred million years ago left thick beds of black basalt near the Crowsnest Pass (right).

Geologists read the province's layer cake of alternating marine and nonmarine sediments (below) like a treasure map.

basins eventually meeting in Colorado about a hundred million years ago. Although this seaway swelled and shrank repeatedly during the Cretaceous, it remained unbroken, keeping the eastern and western halves of North America separated for another thirty-five million years.

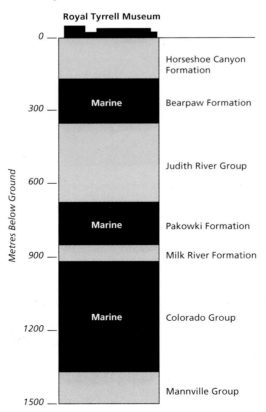

Royal Tyrrell Museum

Metres Below Ground

0	
	Horseshoe Canyon Formation
300	**Marine** — Bearpaw Formation
	Judith River Group
600	
	Marine — Pakowki Formation
900	Milk River Formation
	Marine — Colorado Group
1200	
	Mannville Group
1500	

The sea that bisected North America and covered parts of Alberta was warm and shallow. Probably no more than three hundred metres deep with temperatures as balmy as fifteen to twenty-five degrees Celsius, the seaway directly shaped the character of the land. Given its enormous size, the seaway naturally acted as a centre for storms and hurricanes. Its warmth invited a moist subtropical climate, which in turn nourished shoreline forests of broad-leaved trees including magnolias, figs and an ancestor of the lichi-nut.

The sediment that poured into the sea from the western mountains also left a legacy of gumbo—grey and brown muds and shales sprinkled with volcanic ash. In the spring and autumn, this Cretaceous muck can make for hazardous off-road driving in Alberta.

As alien seas mixed their salty waters on Alberta's plains, volcanoes erupted in the Crowsnest Pass region of southeastern British Columbia. Travellers driving along Highway 3 west of Coleman can see evidence of their ashen spill in a jumbled sequence of massive green and grey rocks. Known as the Crowsnest Volcanics, these rocks contain large crystals of sparkling feldspar and garnet visible to the eye. Geologists haven't yet

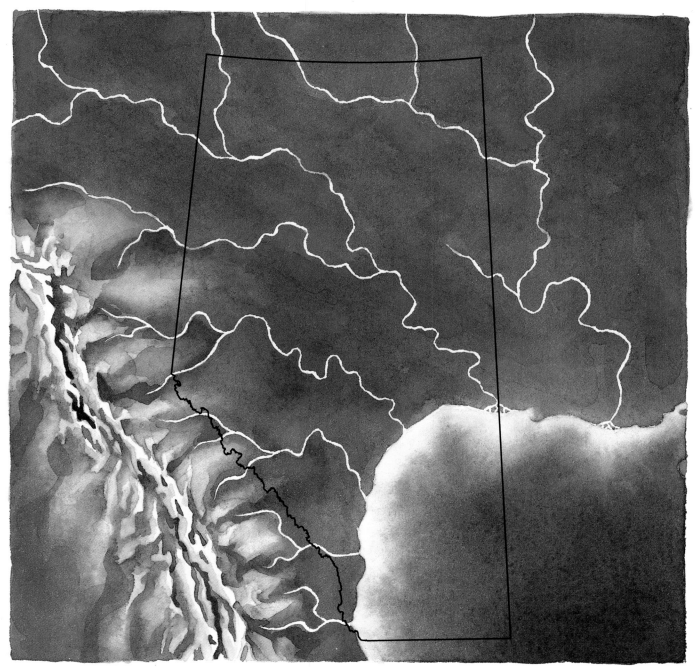

found the volcanoes that made these minerals because sheets of uplifted stone probably buried their creator as terranes continued to collide with western Canada in the Cretaceous and early Tertiary periods.

All this geological activity left a revealing layer cake of alternating marine and nonmarine sediments across the province that geologists read like treasure maps. The marine formations speak directly of the work of Mediterraneanlike seas while the land-laid layers record the presence of evergladelike

swamps and coastal plains. Some layers suggest sandy beaches while others hint at muddy shorelines; some seem defined by wet weather and others by dry spells. And all are amply displayed in the province's southern and central river valleys.

If an army of geologists dug a two-kilometre-deep trench in the ground outside the Royal Tyrrell Museum of Palaeontology, the bottom of this layer cake would begin with the Mannville Group. Composed of sandstones, siltstones, coal and shales, the Mannville

Late Cretaceous Alberta: A swampy lowland located along the western coast of a continental seaway.

63

Sculpted by wind, rain and cold, the haunting hoodoos of the eighty-million-year-old Milk River Formation stand like giant mushrooms (above).

Grey sandstones at Dinosaur Provincial Park speak of ancient meandering rivers (below).

Group left its mark before the great seaway was fully established and when rivers ran north to the Arctic. The group is justifiably famous for its oil sand and heavy oil deposits in Fort McMurray, Cold Lake and Lloydminster. Although the origin of the oil is uncertain, it may have seeped up from underlying Palaeozoic limestones or been cooked in surrounding Cretaceous rocks. Mannville's sticky tarlike oil sands represent almost 1.3 billion barrels of oil, a volume almost equivalent to Alberta's Palaeozoic oil reserves.

The next layer, the Colorado Group, is composed of brown and grey shales and records the initial union of the Arctic Ocean and the Gulf of Mexico. Above this layer lies the eighty-million-year-old Milk River Formation, which is represented by spooky puppetlike hoodoos in Writing-On-Stone Provincial Park. Originally deposited on a shallow marine shelf, its grey and yellow sandstones were later carved by wind and rain into haunting mushroom shapes. Ancient stone drawings, or petroglyphs, made by the Black-

foot and their ancestors add to the mystery of this arid landscape.

Next comes the Pakowki Formation, a thin sequence of drab grey marine shales. Above it lies the seventy-five-million-year-old Judith River Group, a package of earthy sandstones

and mud rock that speaks of ancient rivers, dense swamps, teeming estuaries and a dazzling array of creatures large and small. Dinosaur Provincial Park, a World Heritage Site and one of the richest dinosaur graveyards on Earth, dramatically reveals this special time in the badlands.

The Bearpaw Formation overlies the Judith River Group and records a time nearly seventy-four to seventy-two million years ago when the shallow continental sea, alive with ammonites and sharks, covered much of Alberta. Rocks along the Red Deer River southeast of Drumheller show off this ancient marine environment.

Last but not least comes the fossil-rich Edmonton Group, which lies exposed around the Royal Tyrrell Museum of Palaeontology. In Midland and Dry Island Buffalo Jump provincial parks, the Edmonton Group is characterized by alternating beds of coal, sandstone and mudstone. The group records the story of a land shifting from a swampy coastal plain to a plain of rivers and forests as

the seaway beat its last retreat from Alberta seventy-two to sixty-five million years ago.

The Whitemud and Battle formations are two of the most persistent geological markers in southern Alberta's layer cake. Although both formations stand less than twenty metres thick, they prominently cap the valley edge at Horseshoe Canyon and crop out along the Red Deer River north of Drumheller. The Whitemud, named after its bright appearance on sunny summer days, records the presence of shallow, sluggish and meandering streams. But the Battle, or Blackmud as geologists often call it, holds a stacked sequence of volcanic ash beds scattered across wet lowlands and in large lakes throughout southern Alberta. Both layers reflect a time when little sediment washed the land and much volcanic ash coated it. Careful examination of microfossils in the Battle Formation suggests a cool climate, perhaps the product of volcanic dust blocking the sun's rays.

The ebbing and flooding of seas over Alberta that helped create this layer cake was

The remains of the Atlas Coal Mine at East Coulee in the Drumheller valley stand as a reminder of how much of the province's wealth has been tied to geological circumstance.

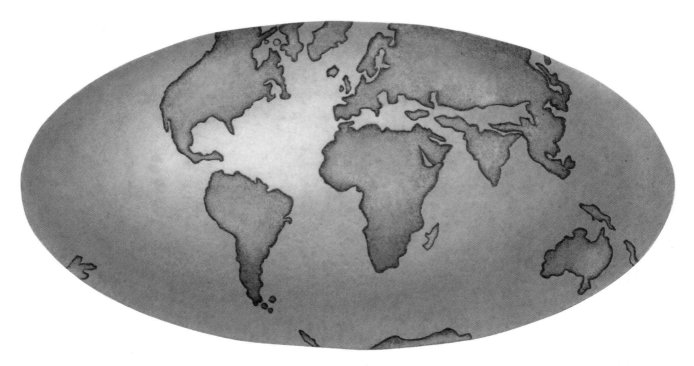

The perpetual continental waltz continued in the Cretaceous with North America on a southwestward drift toward its modern position (above).

Flowering plants (below) added new colour to Cretaceous landscapes.

influenced by several global events including the time-honoured continental waltz. The two mega-landmasses, Laurasia and Gondwana, continued to rip apart, and by the dawn of the Cretaceous, South America was pulling away from Africa while North America continued its divorce from the combined continents of Greenland and Europe. Antarctica and Australia, too, said goodbye to Africa and South America. In the midst of these partings, India slowly drifted northward on a solitary collision course with Asia.

The continental separations helped create new ocean basins that soon flooded the land with shallow seas, accounting for Alberta's periodic floodings. Sea levels continued to rise during the middle of the Cretaceous, eventually cresting at 250 metres above current levels. Vast shallow seas, in which ammonites prospered, became beds for limey oozes in lower latitudes. Today, they form huge chalk deposits in Kansas and Britain that lend their name to the Cretaceous Period (*Creta* is Latin for "chalk").

Smaller continents, larger oceans and new oceanic pathways changed both Alberta's and the earth's weather. During the Cretaceous Period, warm temperatures and tropical conditions made the climate highly hospitable. Pleasant equatorial currents even transformed the poles into green places with lakes and forests.

During all of this pulling and flooding, animals and plants became isolated on drifting continents that served as separate versions of Noah's Ark. About a hundred million years

ago, North America, too, went its own way as it lost its Greenland bridge with Europe when the two continents parted company. But in its place, a new connection appeared, linking northwestern North America with northeastern

Asia. This land bridge, which humans would later use, explains why vast dinosaur graveyards in Alberta and China yield similar finds.

Flowering Plants

As snakes, salamanders, diving birds and social insects established a presence, flowering plants began to dramatically colour the landscape. Angiosperms include a host of modern flora including grasses, dandelions, shrubs and bushes, as well as broad-leaved trees such as oaks, elms and willows. Prior to the ascendancy of angiosperms, the land was carpeted green with needle-leaved gymnosperms. But

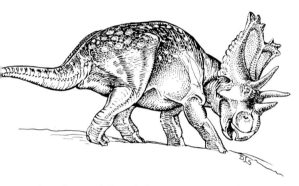

by the middle of the Cretaceous, flowering plants had made sizable inroads and thereafter quickly spread, ultimately dominating the land.

Flowering plants made true evolutionary history. Not only did they grow and reproduce faster than ferns, cycads and gymnosperms, but they also recovered more quickly after being trampled or munched on by dinosaurs. Their brilliant flowers and fruits attracted insect pollinators and hungry planteaters alike, ensuring efficient reproduction and seed dispersal. Given their new popularity, flowering plants soon warded off overattentive herbivores by arming and protecting themselves with a variety of thorns, coarse bark, minerals and chemical poisons (alkyloids). These novel adaptations, in turn, triggered evolutionary responses from assorted plant munchers, such as jaws with beaks and teeth suitable for grinding and grazing. By the end of the Cretaceous, a world once

dotted by evergreens had surrendered to the advance of fast-growing scrub brush and broad-leaved trees mixed with conifers. A modern landscape, or at least one recognizable to humans, had begun to take shape.

Evidence of prosperous plant life in Cretaceous Alberta can be found in the more than one hundred coal mines that once echoed the sounds of picks and drills throughout the Drumheller valley. At the turn of the century, the draw of ready coal profits settled and peopled the Red Deer valley, but the boom was to last a mere fifty years. The coal beds that Joseph Burr Tyrrell spied in 1884 began their geological odyssey seventy-two million years ago as Cretaceous peat bogs along the shores of the Alberta seaway. As this shallow sea expanded and contracted over hundreds of thousands of years, accompanying peat swamps moved about the province. These migrations partly explain why Cretaceous coal beds occur from the foothills to the prairies and from central Alberta to the American border.

Cretaceous plant-eating dinosaurs came in a wide assortment of kinds including well-armoured ankylosaurs (above), horned ceratopsians (middle) and dome-headed pachycephalosaurs (below).

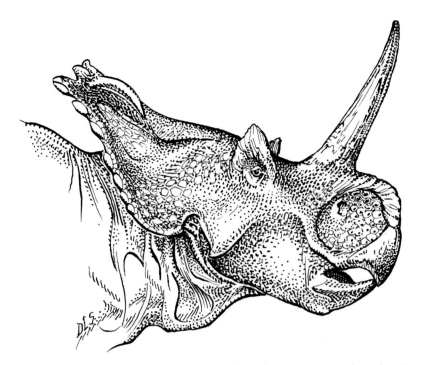

Another hypothesis proposes that the sauropods, accustomed to feeding on tall gymnosperms, just couldn't switch to the new low-growing plants colonizing the land. Whatever the reason, dinosaur herbivores such as duck-billed hadrosaurs, frilled ceratopsians, armoured ankylosaurs and dome-headed pachycephalosaurs eclipsed the long-necks and had their day in the Cretaceous sun 140–65 million years ago.

But as the planteaters diversified so, too, did the meateaters. Evolutionary trends in the Cretaceous favoured the appearance of a

Beauty marks: Planteaters, such as *Centrosaurus* (above), *Styracosaurus* (middle) and *Corythosaurus* (below), probably used their odd-shaped horns, frills and crests for sexual displays, defence or communication.

One hypothesis suggests that the Cretaceous debut of flowering plants may also be linked to the remarkable diversity of dinosaur herbivores that lived along Alberta's coastal plains. It may somehow explain why the giant sauropods such as the long-necked *Apatosaurus* faltered and went into decline. Some palaeontologists suggest that the regenerative and reproductive powers of flowering plants favoured the evolution of many new species of dinosaurs.

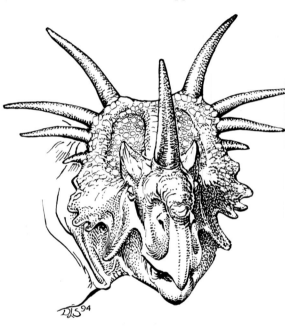

host of small carnivorous dinosaurs, many of which were probably functionally superior to their Jurassic counterparts. As tall as humans, toothless dinosaurs like *Struthiomimus* (ostrich-mimic) and *Ornithomimus* (bird-mimic) may have helped to clean up after a messy tyrannosaur feed or, in turn, may have dined on the organisms scavenging the rotting remains.

Cretaceous Adaptations

There were other amazing changes. The startling array of headgear among planteaters—including crests, frills and horns—suggests that these creatures behaved in complex ways within and perhaps between species. Studies of hadrosaurs show that some of these socia-

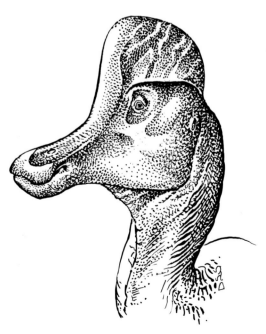

ble swamp dwellers were capable of vocalizing in the form of hoots or honks. The dome-headed pachycephalosaurs, the big-horn sheep of their day, used their domed heads in butting contests to establish dominance.

The small carnivores, such as velociraptors, were stealthy and clever predators thanks to their large brains, forward-directed eyes, long ostrichlike legs, vicious claws and grasping hands. But the ever-present tyrannosaurs, which thrived until the great extinction, still remind palaeontologists that ultimately might was right in the Cretaceous.

Tracks in the Past

In 1979, the Bennett Dam flooded one of the most unusual dinosaur sites in western Canada. Beneath the reservoir created by the dam are thousands of dinosaur tracks and trackways trapped in black shales of the Gething Formation. Before the dam was completed palaeontologists from the Provincial Museum of Alberta collected and documented these dinosaur pathways. They jackhammered tracks and trackways free of the shale and made latex and fiberglass casts of tracks that could not be removed. They also extensively photographed and mapped the area.

The result of their work is a unique portrait of dinosaur life in western Canada 110 million years ago.

The site contains at least five different kinds of track-makers including dinosaurs, birds and possibly a mammal. It also contains the earliest record of duck-billed hadrosaurs and ceratopsians as well as the oldest known tracks of birds. The evidence suggests that communities of planteaters moved along the shores of the early Cretaceous inland sea, pausing to browse but always on guard against large meateaters. Shorebirds worked the coastline, probing the rippled and muddy shore for worms and other grubs. Interestingly, scientists found no tracks of sauropods, suggesting that these giant dinosaurs preferred southern climes.

Approximately twenty dinosaur track and trackway sites, ranging in age from early to

Using its impressive head-gear as a sound device or a horn, *Lambeosaurus* (left) inhabited swampy basins.

The polished shales of the Gething Formation along the Peace River captured the tracks of a wandering carnivore (below).

When populated by "terrible lizards," Dinosaur Provincial Park was a lush coastal plain (above).

Teeth (below) make up some of the oldest identifiable dinosaur remains in the province.

late Cretaceous, dot the province. Tracks in the Gates Formation near Grand Cache reveal many of the same kinds of footprints as those in British Columbia but have received little scientific attention. Other sites in southwestern and south central Alberta offer tantalizing glimpses of dinosaur walkabouts.

The Milk River Formation, however, has yielded the oldest identifiable dinosaur bones and teeth from Alberta. In Verdegris Coulee, near Writing-On-Stone Provincial Park, a sparse collection of fossils reflects an eighty-million-year-old dinosaur community of duck-billed hadrosaurs, ceratopsians, small and large meateaters and armoured ankylosaurs. Although the genera and species changed, these kinds of dinosaurs roamed Alberta for fifteen million years until the end of the Mesozoic Era.

Verdegris Coulee has yielded even more important remains: the fossilized teeth of Cretaceous mammals collected by Dr. R.C. Fox of the University of Alberta. These fossils are critical to scientists studying the evolution of mammals and their existence in a world dominated by dinosaurs. Known almost exclusively from fossil teeth, early mammal groups have names based on tooth shape. Hence palaeontologists speak of triconodonts, symmetrodonts, multituberculates and tribotheres as well as the better known marsupials and placentals.

The mammals that scurried about Cretaceous Alberta were probably small and secretive. But along with the rodentlike multituberculates and pouched marsupials, a new family member appeared—the eutherian, or placental. The placentals possessed a special nutritive organ, the placenta, that developed in the mother to nourish the embryo. The placenta allowed the fetus to remain within the mother's body and to grow to an advanced form before birth. Although placental mammals are common today (mice, cats, monkeys and humans), they remained almost inconspicuous in the Cretaceous until the egg-laying dinosaurs died out.

Cretaceous Park

No place on Earth yields the remains of so many individual skeletons representing so many different kinds of dinosaurs as the rocks of the Judith River Group in Dinosaur Provincial Park. No place on Earth attracts so many different scientists interested in dinosaurs and assorted wonders such as dinosaurs' skin impressions, stomach contents and social relationships. Since Tyrrell's day, more than thirty-six different species of dinosaurs have been found in the park's eroding badlands. The dry and washed-out land has yielded another eighty-four species of vertebrates including fish, salamanders, frogs, crocodiles, champsosaurs and mammals. The remains of clams, snails and plants are also abundant, indicating that a green coastal plain, much like northern Florida, once occupied a place that is now almost desert.

Perhaps the Park's most spectacular site is a large ceratopsian graveyard. Located in the heart of the Park, the *Centrosaurus* bone bed covers an area the size of a football field. Here, more than 220 individuals lie as a community united in death.

Working like detectives at the scene of a mass murder, researchers have concluded that the centrosaurs died simultaneously, probably during a flood. Meateaters such as *Albertosaurus* then picked the carcasses clean. Another

flood redistributed the bones and buried them in their final resting place to be uncovered seventy-five million years later. Such evidence suggests that ceratopsian dinosaurs gathered in great herds for at least part of the year as they searched for new feeding or breeding grounds.

An American expedition to the Gobi Desert officially discovered the first dinosaur eggs in the 1920s—a find that then probably seemed bizarre and unlikely. Today, hundreds of eggs have been recovered in France, China and North America. The Royal Tyrrell Museum of Palaeontology made the first Canadian discovery of whole dinosaur eggs in 1987 at Devil's Coulee. Here bedrock pokes out of the ranchland along the Milk River Ridge north of the Montana border. The Devil's Coulee eggs date to the same time as

Hypacrosaur mothers (above), whose heads would rise above the average kitchen ceiling, remarkably cared for small hatchlings (below) that could fit into two human hands.

In the shallow Bearpaw Sea (above right), which submerged most of southern Alberta, mosasaurs (above left) left their teeth marks on the shells of ammonites (below), their favourite food.

the remains in Dinosaur Provincial Park, but the geology of the coulee tells a different story. During Cretaceous summers in southwestern Alberta, ephemeral and shallow rivers flowed eastward across an arid but forested plain. Although seasonal floods unloaded sheets of muddy sandy silt upon the land, vegetation quickly reclaimed the floodplain. In this area, large groups of hypacrosaur duck-billed dinosaurs gathered to mate, nest and hatch their eggs. The parents protected their tiny hatchlings from predators until the young were old enough to move on their own. Eggs found in clusters, fragments of embryonic dinosaur bone and thousands of pieces of eggshell all suggest that Devil's Coulee was at one time a dinosaur rookery.

Life in the Bearpaw

The fossil record indicates that sea life in Cretaceous Alberta was just as diverse and hazardous as life on land. The shallow sea that periodically bathed Alberta during the Cretaceous advanced over the southern half of the province one last time seventy-four to seventy-two million years ago. Named after the Bearpaw Mountains in Montana, where geologists first recognized its existence, the

Bearpaw Sea was home to swimming reptiles, ammonites, squids, clams, oysters, lobsters, shrimp and fish. Due to the flatness of the land, the Bearpaw Sea advanced across three hundred kilometres of low-relief coastal plain in less than one million years. It drowned forests and swamps, turning what is now Medicine Hat and Lethbridge into a huge shallow bay with a network of wetlands.

In the Bearpaw, sharks, marine turtles and plesiosaurs dined on fish while giant lizard-like mosasaurs pursued coiled and straight ammonites. Judging by the abundance of tooth-punctured ammonite shells, mosasaurs favoured these creatures as a delicacy.

Plesiosaurs came in two varieties—short-necked pliosaurs and long-necked elasmosaurs.

Flying through water with penguinlike paddles, plesiosaurs diligently fished Alberta's ancient estuaries.

Both forms could "fly" through the water using their paddles in a manner similar to that of penguins. The remains of plesiosaurs have been found in ancient estuary deposits in southern Alberta, indicating that they occasionally swam upstream, perhaps to lay eggs or rid themselves of marine parasites.

The Bearpaw Sea began its retreat from Alberta seventy-two million years ago. But it periodically reflooded its old haunts, drowning southern Alberta for thousands of years. The geological feature known as the Drumheller Marine Tongue tells of one spectacular reflooding that is exposed along the Drumheller valley edge at Horsethief Canyon, just west of the Royal Tyrrell Museum of Palaeontology. The yellow marine sands at Horsethief Canyon yield the fossils of oysters and clams left by surging storms in the shallow sea.

As the Bearpaw Sea withdrew its watery embraces from Alberta, swamps, coastal deltas and river plains advanced toward the south and east. As a consequence, land-based creatures and flowering plants returned in great numbers. Most of these animals looked very similar to those found in the Judith River Group at Dinosaur Provincial Park. There were, however, a few exceptions, particularly among the planteaters. In the swamps, a new array of duck-bills now foraged including the giant *Edmontosaurus* and its more modern-looking cousin *Saurolophus* as well as ceratopsians including *Arrhinoceratops*. The large and small predators such as *Albertosaurus* and *Dromaeosaurus* remained basically unchanged. These meateaters continued to terrorize other dinosaurs just as they had when they appeared on the scene two million years earlier.

Heading for Extinction

Nearly sixty-seven million years ago, this stable picture of lush forests enlivened by honking duck-bills, screeching birds and sudden death started to change as global and local climates became drier and cooler. As southern Alberta's climate came to resemble that of modern New Mexico, the diversity of dinosaurs diminished. The fossil record suggests that during the last two million years of the Cretaceous, sixty-seven to sixty-five million years ago, dramatic forces had been unleashed. An assemblage of bones collected from the Scollard Formation between Red Deer and Drumheller includes two of the most celebrated dinosaurs—*Tyrannosaurus rex* and *Triceratops albertensis*. Compared with the

Existing just sixty-five million years ago, *Triceratops* (right) was one of the last dinosaurs to flourish before the great extinction.

The duck-billed *Edmontosaurus* (below) may have had a balloonlike tissue in its large nostrils to make sounds.

seventy-five-million-year-old Judith River Group, this collection contains one-quarter as many kinds of meat-eating dinosaurs and about one-half as many kinds of planteaters. The seventy-million-year-old Horseshoe Canyon Formation appears to support this trend: although the overall number of dinosaurs is just a bit smaller than in the Judith River Group, there are clearly fewer kinds of meateaters. To palaeontologists, who argue about the significance of these differences, the loss in diversity suggests that dinosaurs were headed toward extinction before other calamities struck.

Geologists generally agree that one or several large asteroids hit the earth sixty-five million years ago. They do not agree, however, about the short- and long-term effects of the bombardment and whether its nuclearlike fallout led to the demise of the dinosaurs and caused many other Cretaceous extinctions. Scientists, in fact, regard the asteroid crash or crashes and the entire issue of the extinctions as two separate events that may or may not be related.

Ken and Marion Knudsen's *T. rex* Ranch north of Tolman Bridge along the Red Deer River has played a role in this important debate. Perched atop sediments of the Scollard Formation—the last record of the age of dinosaurs in Alberta—the ranch gave up a partial skeleton of *Tyrannosaurus rex* in 1981. The ranch also contains exposures of Cretaceous-Tertiary boundary clay, and almost every year the Knudsens patiently watch as geologists from all over the world come to collect samples and view evidence that might explain what happened to the dinosaurs.

In 1993, a fifty-metre-wide block of prairie dropped ten metres during the spring runoff to reveal the best exposure of the Cretaceous-Tertiary boundary in Canada. Royal Tyrrell Museum geologists Dave Eberth and Dennis Braman, leading a field trip to the area for the Geological Association of Canada, were fascinated by the slump scar. Although the freshly exposed boundary clay was only two to three centimetres thick, it showed an organized structure with a lower tan and upper dark layer. Recognized in boundary clay layers elsewhere in the United States, these two layers may represent a short-term ejecta (the lower tan layer) caused by the explosive impact of an asteroid and a longer-term fireball (the upper dark layer) caused by weeks and months of fallout of fine ash that would have circled the earth after the collision.

Abundant evidence for an asteroid collision lies in the clay. The platinum group element iridium, an element common in asteroids, enriches the upper layer. Grains of shocked quartz that show numerous fracture lines caused by intense pressure are also present. The lower layer contains microspherules of altered glass formed from melted rock as it was blown through the atmosphere and cooled. Numerous other features, such as the presence of the minerals stishovite and magnesioferrite, also hint at the clay's extraterrestrial origin.

In the last twelve years, hundreds of scientific papers have speculated on the catastroph-

ic effects of an asteroid collision on earth. The more popular and gloomy scenarios include months and years of dust-enshrouded darkness, freezing global temperatures, acid rain, deafening shock waves, wrenching tidal waves and scorching wildfires that burned the northern hemisphere to a crisp. Creatures unfortunate enough to be within a few thousand kilometres of the bombardment site perished or suffered terribly. But the long-term effects of such an impact are difficult to predict. The extent and length of the devastation depends not only on the size of the asteroid but the angle of its impact and the type of rock vaporized by the crash.

Based upon the amount of iridium found

Although known from less than twelve complete skeletons, *Tyrannosaurus rex* (left) is easily the world's most popular carnivore.

Geologists take turns at collecting the Cretaceous-Tertiary boundary clay at the bottom of a black coal seam in the Red Deer River valley (below).

With its lathlike fractures, a grain of shocked quartz provides partial evidence of an asteroid bombardment sixty-five million years ago.

in the Cretaceous-Tertiary boundary clay, scientists conclude that the asteroid may have been ten kilometres in diameter, and its speed upon impact may have been in the range of two hundred thousand kilometres per hour. Such an otherwordly propellant would have created a crater one hundred to two hundred kilometres wide and twenty to forty kilometres deep. The energy released from such a collision would have been a thousand times more powerful than the detonation of all the world's nuclear weapons at once. However, such a cataclysm would not have extinguished all life on Earth. Different ecosystems would have suffered or endured the impact in different ways. Some would have vanished while others would have recovered over time, and a few may not have been grossly affected at all.

At a recent geological conference held in Edmonton to discuss the Cretaceous-Tertiary boundary extinctions, scientists were presented with data revealing that the pattern of extinctions among different kinds of plants, invertebrates and vertebrates around the world did not lend itself to simple explanations. In fact, most scientists now believe that no single mass extinction took place. They propose instead that there may have been a series of extinctions, some gradual and some rapid, all clustered around the boundary. Plants, for example, show important changes before and after the boundary. Marine invertebrates such as tiny globular foraminifera show changes hundreds of thousands of years before the boundary and after it. Mammals had begun diversifying before the boundary. Dinosaurs were probably in decline before the asteroid struck (but evidence is still being gathered). Other creatures such as crocodiles and birds appear unscathed by the boundary event. Scientists also know that global climates had cooled prior to the collision and that sea levels had fallen, exposing greater masses of land and allowing previously restricted creatures the opportunity to mingle.

Such complexities do not disprove the asteroid hypothesis, but they do emphasize that ecological and evolutionary changes were well in progress before, during and after the impact. The fatal bombardment clearly changed the lives of many plants and animals already struggling to cope in a rapidly changing world. But the collision and its aftermath may have been the straw that broke the dinosaur's back rather than the sole cause of its demise.

Scientists currently estimate that sixty to eighty percent of all living species went extinct

VAL HERMAN

by the end of the Cretaceous. Dinosaurs, pterosaurs, plesiosaurs and mosasaurs all became the stuff of bone fields. So, too, did a few mammals. Among the invertebrates, ammonites and a variety of clams, including reef-forming rudists, disappeared forever. Most birds, fish, mammals, turtles, crocodiles, lizards, snakes, frogs and salamanders survived the cataclysm to prosper until modern times.

Perhaps the only certainty about the Cretaceous extinction and its related asteroid bombardment is that scientists will continue to argue for a long time to come about why *Tyrannosaurus rex* and his cousins disappeared.

Alien bombardment: The energy released from the impact of an asteroid ten kilometres in diameter had impressive consequences— an explosion a thousand times more powerful than all of the world's nuclear weapons.

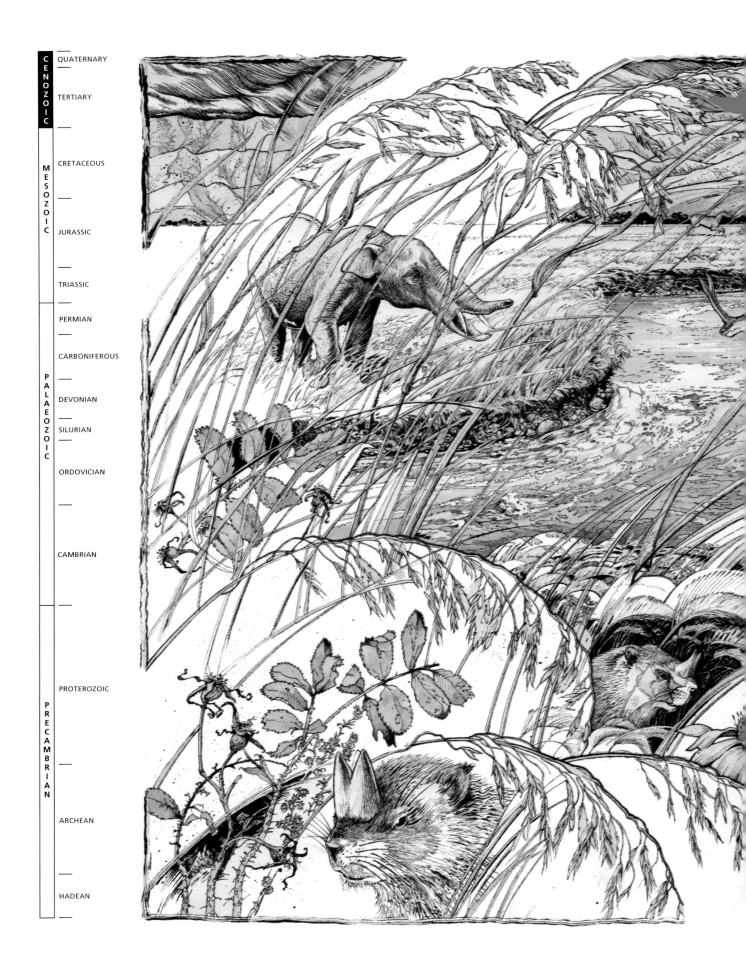

CENOZOIC

QUATERNARY

TERTIARY

MESOZOIC

CRETACEOUS

JURASSIC

TRIASSIC

PERMIAN

CARBONIFEROUS

PALAEOZOIC

DEVONIAN

SILURIAN

ORDOVICIAN

CAMBRIAN

PROTEROZOIC

PRECAMBRIAN

ARCHEAN

HADEAN

Bearlike tillodonts, placental pioneers, flourished briefly during the Cenozoic and then gave way to other mammals.

Chapter Six

The Cenozoic Cooling

Long ago, the Blackfoot so admired the Rocky Mountains that they gave each lofty peak a name: Little Chief, Mad Wolf, Going-to-the-Sun, Four Bears and Almost-a-Dog. They aptly referred to the entire mountain chain, however, as the Backbone of the World. Although the creation of this backbone properly started in the late Jurassic, its true birth occurred during the Cenozoic, the era of recent life.

The lengthy making of the Rocky Mountain backbone was partly the product of island arcs colliding with the West Coast, a process that had by now cobbled together Vancouver Island and the Coast Mountains. But as the huge Pacific oceanic plate butted against the western margin of North America, the banging and thrusting of rock became more dramatic. As the plate split in two, its southern part sank under the western edge of the United States while a northern piece moved northeast, dragging and tearing against Canada's fringes, eventually sinking under Alaska. For more than thirty million years, grinding, folding and lifting defined the geo-

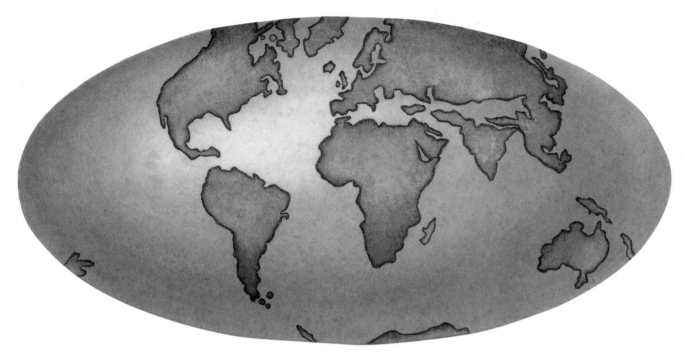

About twenty million years ago, the continents drifted into familiar-looking positions (above).

The dragging and tearing of part of the Pacific Plate against western Canada caused volcanic eruptions (whose locations are indicated by triangles below) across British Columbia.

logical destiny of western Canada as new mountains rose and were pushed farther eastward into Alberta. These collisions predictably ruptured the crust, and new volcanoes appeared in British Columbia's interior. Tectonic pressures also thrust up layers of western Canada's ancient sea floor, which had turned to rock after being buried for millions of years. As these slabs played leapfrog, jagged peaks emerged along the British Columbia and Alberta border. Alberta's backbone had taken its place in the world as part of the great cordillera, which gracefully runs the length of North America.

The making of mountains, however, was not an isolated Cenozoic event. Around the world, continental collisions created backbones of varying heights and sizes. When India began colliding with southern Asia about fifty-five million years ago, the spectacular Himalayas rose to heights above four kilometres. Africa bumped into southern Europe, creating mountains in northern Africa, the Adriatic and Italy. Elsewhere, the crust continued to tear as Australia continued to move away from Antarctica, and Saudia Arabia began to drift away from Africa. And so the modern world took familiar shape and form.

The Cenozoic, which spans sixty-five million years to the modern day, has two distinct periods: the Tertiary and Quaternary. The Tertiary witnessed the evolutionary triumph of birds and mammals, the making of western Canada's backbone and the great climatic cooling of the planet. Comprising most of

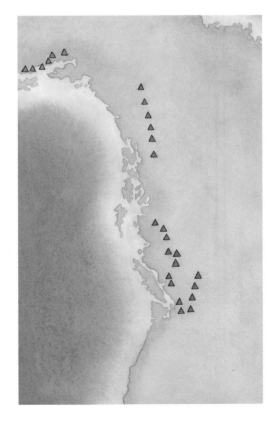

Cenozoic time, the Tertiary did not yield to the Quaternary until 1.8 million years ago. As the shortest period in geologic time, the Quaternary is a geological sentence without a period; no one knows how long it will last or how it will end. But the youthful Quaternary has already lived a full life, having witnessed a bewildering array of extinctions, flowing ice sheets and roving bands of humans.

Mammals of the Tertiary

During the first ten million years of the Tertiary, Alberta remained a continuous car-pet of evergreen forests and bush punctuated by rivers, lakes, marshes and swamps. With a high year-round rainfall and tropical temperatures ranging between twenty and twenty-five degrees Celsius, the province probably resembled modern-day Louisiana.

In this landscape, a variety of creatures flourished. Freed from the tyranny of dinosaurs, mammals especially began to diversify on a grand scale. The fossils of rodentlike multituberculates and insect-eating placentals have been found in the Paskapoo Formation as well as Saskatchewan's Ravenscrag Formation. Marsupials left North America by the

Plesiadapis (above) was an early primate, the group that includes monkeys and humans.

From forms such as *Hyopsodus* (below)–a primitive condylarth–eventually came all hoofed animals.

middle of the Tertiary, and only the opossum ventured back from South America, a warm refuge for pouched mammals. Other fossil finds include the ancestors of several primitive primates, modern hedgehogs, shrews and bats.

Condylarths, ancestors of hoofed mammals, were also frequent prowlers of Alberta's ancient Tertiary forests. Early kinds were dog-sized and munched on leafy plants as well as some meat. From the condylarths came all modern hoofed mammals including cattle, deer and sheep as well as horses, tapirs and rhinoceroses. Even elephants can be traced back to leaf-eating condylarths.

To feed on these vegetarians, meateaters appeared with specialized shearing teeth that worked to slice the flesh of their prey. These predators included the now extinct creodonts, and carnivores such hyaenas, cats, dogs and bears.

Creodonts, such as the weasel-like *Sinopa* (left), and true carnivores, such as *Miacis* (below), were among the first successful flesh-eating mammals of intermediate size.

Tertiary Landscapes

In the middle of the Tertiary, as the Canadian Rockies lifted the land, the Bearpaw Sea finally drained south out of Alberta and Saskatchewan. Next, geology's ever-present assistant, erosion, began to play with the plains. From the mountains, sheets of sediment were carried onto the plains by braided rivers, particularly when tectonic uplifts made the Rockies even more imposing. Some of these sediments were preserved while erosion and, in particular, glacial advances later stripped away most others.

Because of this extensive glacial erosion, only a few scattered remnants of middle to late Tertiary rock remain in the province. Not surprisingly, this yellowish rock caps the

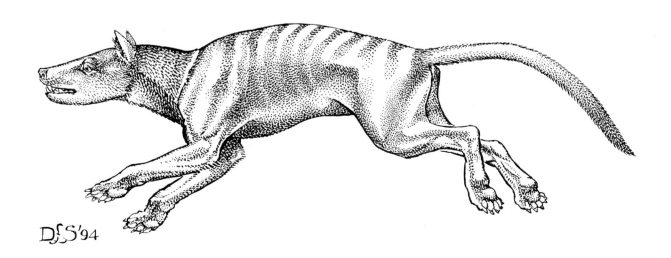

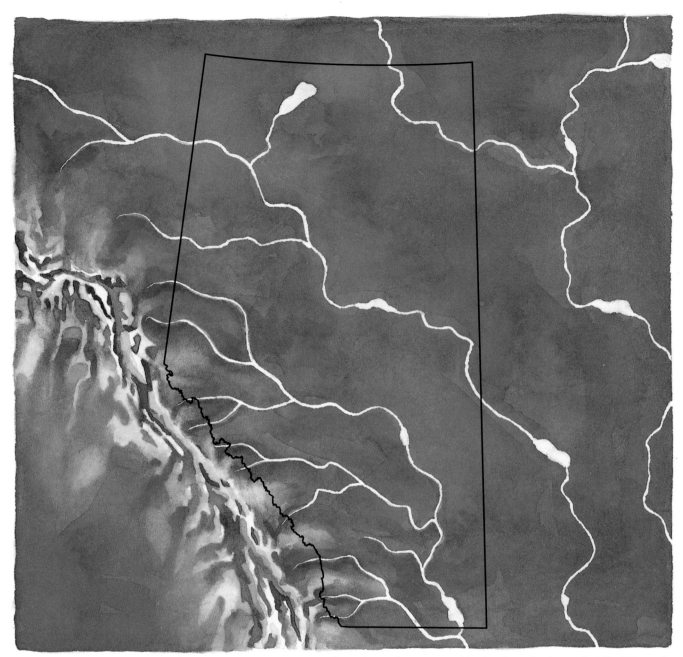

Cenozoic Alberta: A grassy land with a rocky western border, north-south flowing rivers and boggy wetlands.

province's hills and consists of sands and gravels (prime construction materials) thirty to forty and three to ten million years old. The rock on these Tertiary "islands" is often called by its geographic place name: the Hand Hills Formation, the Cypress Hills Formation, the Swan Hills Gravels and the Saddle Hills Gravels.

Most of this rock was deposited by fast-moving sandy rivers that flowed north and east across steep plains stretching out from the mountains. As the mountains rose in the southwest, they eventually cast a rain shadow over this land, reducing rainfall. Through time, extensive wetlands characteristic of the early Tertiary gave way to drier riverine woodlands made up of alder, oak, walnut and elm. For the remainder of the Tertiary, drier and cooler weather prevailed, encouraging the forests to recede and grasses to advance. Over millions of years, the province came to resemble a modern African savanna.

Fossils from the Cypress Hills Formation in southeastern Alberta and especially southwestern Saskatchewan indicate just how dramatically life had changed since the opening

A forty-million-year-old rhinoceros jawbone from the Cypress Hills (left).

Outcrops of Cenozoic rock lie mostly in the south western part of the province (below) with a few scattered islands in south central and eastern Alberta.

of the Tertiary. In this forty-two- to thirty-five-million-year-old formation, geologists have recovered the skeletal remains of birds, snakes, turtles, amphibians, fish and a host of large and small mammals. The mammal collection alone comprises almost a hundred different species including several kinds of animals new to western Canada. Among them are mice, flying lemurs, bats, rabbits, primitive horses and rhinoceroses. Perhaps the strangest mammals in this lot include giant piglike entelodonts and brontotheres. The former may have used bony cheek and jaw protuberances for display and combat. The latter sported a diverging pair of mysterious bony growths where rhinoceroses carry a horn.

Primitive horses the size of large dogs have also been found in the Cypress Hills. In many ways the evolution of the horse, originally a North American native, reflects the Tertiary's ecological history. The beast first emerged nearly fifty million years ago as a forest dweller and leaf browser the size of a fox. As the climate cooled and the forests receded, its descendants increased in size, reduced the number of toes from three to one, lengthened their legs and developed good chewing teeth with infolded enamel. As these changes took place, a fast-running and highly efficient grazing animal emerged that was well suited for life on grasslands.

The Handhills Formation in south central Alberta provides another glimpse of late Tertiary life about fourteen million years ago. Its ancient sands and gravels near Drumheller

speak of the comings and goings of herds of horses, numerous rodents and camels (another North American stalwart that later immigrated to Asia). Fossil collections of similar age in Wood Mountain, Saskatchewan, have also yielded primitive pronghorns, pocket mice, hedgehogs, moles, shrews, chipmunks, flying squirrels, beavers and an elephantlike mastodont. Such species certainly traversed Alberta's plains and hills as well. Their amazing diversity hints at another ecological change: the expansion of grass.

During the Cenozoic Era, hardy prairie grasses colonized the plains (right), preparing the way for great herds of horses, camels and eventually buffalo and pronghorns. With their massive root systems, prairie grasses (below) proved resistant to drought and cold.

The Expansion of Grass

Grasses, which cover up to one-third of the earth's land surface, have not only nurtured great herds of mammals but entire human civilizations. Characterized by narrow leaves with parallel veins and small inconspicuous flowers, grasses come in about nine thousand different species. Grasses such as rice, wheat, maize, oats, barley, millet and sorghum remain important staples of the human diet. Not only is grass widespread, but it grows in virtually every environment including the coldest and driest of regions. Grasslands are also referred to as savannas, parklands, prairies or any place where grasses and sedges abound.

The earliest grasses appeared in the early Tertiary but didn't really become a significant and distinctive presence on the land until much later. Grasses don't fossilize well so their history is poorly known. They probably spread across the plains in response to drier and cooler temperatures. True waving grasslands didn't appear in Alberta until about fourteen million years ago.

The success of grass on the world's plains

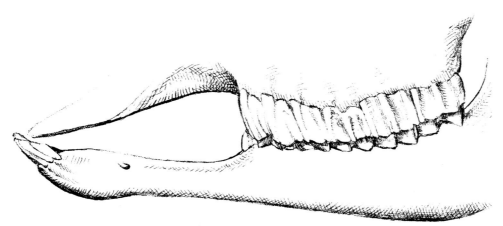

These high-crowned goat's teeth (left) mark mammals' evolutionary dental adaptations to abrasive grasses. The Irish Elk, *Megaloceras* (below), had antlers three metres wide and lived in Europe during the Ice Age.

and savannas owes much to its structure, growth habits and biology. Unlike most plants, grasses do not grow from the tips of their shoots; instead they grow from the base. So, even when grass leaves are damaged, the plant continues to grow. The root system of grasses also ensures their durability: up to ninety percent of the weight of a typical grass plant lies underground, forming a densely tangled root system. Such an underground network helps grasses survive cold and dry spells, raging fires and herds of thundering grass-eaters.

The spread of grasses across the Cenozoic plains greatly influenced the animals that lived there. The silica present in grass leaves is tough and abrasive and explains why grass is among the hardest of plants for animals to chew. In order for mammals to comfortably dine on grass, evolution made several dental adjustments. These changes included high-crowned molars with infolded enamel and the alteration of premolars into molariform teeth, which increased the resistance of teeth to constant grinding.

Before grasses carpeted the plains, vegetarians often escaped predators by darting into a maze of woodlands or ponds. But as Alberta and other areas lost trees and gained grass, herbivores became vulnerable to predators. In response, many groups, such as the horse, camel and bison, slowly developed longer legs to outrun their attackers. Thus, grass gently but unremittingly stirred the expansion and diversity of large hooved mammals.

The cooling that had begun forty million years ago continued well beyond the end of the Tertiary. By then it had already frozen the Arctic Ocean and prepared massive ice sheets

Well adapted to the cold, both the woolly mammoth (above) and woolly rhinoceros (below) had thick hides, small ears and huge molar teeth to chew on coarse tundra plants.

in the world's mountains and Antarctica. All this cooling had much to do with the world's new mountain ranges. The ice ages may have been triggered by the uplift of massive mountain belts such as those in Tibet. As warm monsoons inundated the cool plateau, carbon dioxide was removed from the atmosphere. The progressive loss of this greenhouse gas that helps to keep the climate warm may have triggered glacial advances.

The first great ice sheets conquered North America and Europe almost two million years ago in the early Quaternary when the earth experienced short cool summers and long mild winters. Precipitated by greater winter snowfalls than summer melts, the glaciers grew and slowly advanced over the northern continents from their mountain strongholds or frigid latitudes. Restlessly advancing and then retreating, the kilometre-

thick glacial ice scraped away at the land and transformed what is now present-day Canada into a barren and hilly expanse of frozen water.

North America's greatest ice sheet, the Laurentide, originated near Hudson Bay and covered thirteen million square kilometres. Its frozen fingers even pushed as far south as Montana, Minnesota and New Jersey. When it began to melt some twelve to fifteen thousand years ago, its runoff submerged ninety percent of the prairie in lakes or stagnant ice. Before the grasses returned, the plains went from tundra to forest.

During the Quaternary's deep freezes, ice covered parts of Alberta at least four separate times. The sheets advanced from the Rocky Mountains and Hudson Bay to join hands over the plains. At times, an ice-free gap or corridor ran north and south between these two ice sheets, creating a tenuous refuge for creatures and plants. The corridor also became an important highway, perhaps allowing people from Asia to enter the heart of North America.

A glimpse of ice age life can be found at Welsch Valley in Saskatchewan and Medicine Hat in Alberta. Fossils from Welsch Valley include *Borophagus,* a dog with hyaenalike habits and the mammoth *Mammuthus meridionalis.* Medicine Hat has yielded early Quaternary creatures including mammoths, modern horses and llamas, a form that originally evolved in North America. More recent fossils include a Columbian mammoth, horses, reindeer and the camel. The major predators of the day were the American lion, the short-faced bear and saber-toothed tiger.

The oldest evidence of *Homo sapiens* in North America is approximately seventeen thousand years old and consists of stone tools from the Bluefish Caves in the Yukon. From Siberia, humans crossed the Bering Land Bridge into Alaska and then walked south. For archaeologists, Alberta plays a special role in

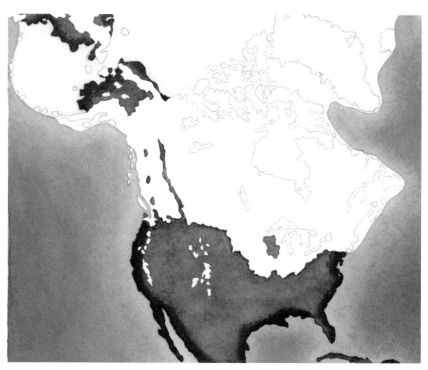

this human invasion of the continent over Alberta's primitive highway. During the last ice age, the ice-free corridor periodically opened and closed from the Yukon along the eastern slopes of the Rocky Mountains and south into Montana. The first human pioneers on the continent likely found this passageway while pursuing game. Archaeologists are still searching for evidence of human beings' early arrival at ice-free corridor sites throughout Alberta and British Columbia. But postglacial erosion and human activity, past and present, have made the search a difficult one.

Flowing from the Canadian Shield and out of the Rockies, great sheets of ice periodically covered Canada during the past 1.8 million years (above). As ice flowed and then retreated, ice-free corridors provided a path into North America from Asia for a variety of animals including humans.

Homo sapiens (below) were fully evolved by the time they entered North America more than seventeen thousand years ago.

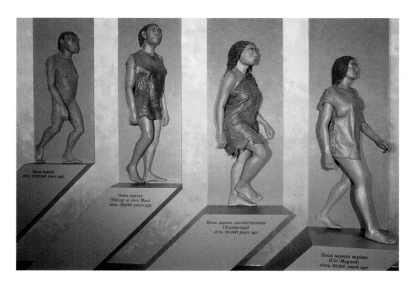

As the glaciers retreated, they left in their wake huge boulders such as the Okotoks erratics (above).

The Columbia Icefields (below) between Banff and Jasper contain the remnants of glaciers that once extended to the Athabasca River.

The movement of sheets of ice across the land left both scars and debris. From parallel striations carved across the Precambrian Shield to pink granite erratic boulders, the evidence of recent glacial activity is preserved around the province. As glacial sheets melted, they also released torrents of water. In the wake of this great melt, huge lakes formed including Glacial Lakes Drumheller, Bassano and McConnell (which partially survives to this day as Great Slave Lake and Lake Athabasca).

The combined forces of melting ice, flowing water and loose sediment reworked the land in powerful ways. Some of Alberta's most conspicuous landscapes have a distinctly glacial look about them. Think of the river valleys of Calgary, Edmonton and Lethbridge, the badlands of Dinosaur and Writing-On-Stone provincial parks, the knob and kettle pasturelands north of Drumheller and countless unnamed sloughs and shallow lakes.

The carnivores and hooved creatures that populated North America at the end of the last glaciation suffered major extinctions from twelve thousand to nine thousand years ago. These disappearances occurred when humans spread throughout North America and the ice sheets retreated to their

mountain or northern homes. Over a span of three thousand years, woolly mammoths, giant beavers almost as big as black bears, the dire wolf (a heavily built version of the timber wolf), ground sloths, sabre-toothed cats, horses and giant bison with horns that spread six feet all vanished. Scientists offer two explanations for the extinction of nearly forty kinds of large mammals on the continent. One theory argues that human hunters exterminated the creatures while another theory holds that rapid environmental transformations forced many species into extinction as the prairies went from glacial bogs to forests to grasslands at a phenomenal rate. Probably both played a role in ending the Age of Mammals. But these extinctions left the plains open for the multiplication of the survivors—the fabled herds of bison, pronghorn and caribou.

Albertans now live during the Holocene Epoch of the Quaternary Period of the Cenozoic Era. It is a time when both the number and behaviour of humans has rapidly changed the character of the land and started another spate of mass extinctions. Like all citizens of Earth, Albertans remain an integral part of an ongoing organic evolution that promises neither heaven nor hell, just more change.

As Albertans play out their destinies on the land, they are in turn transformed by it. No matter how much they might argue about the merits of dams, housing subdivisions and power lines, the earth will patiently record the prudent or wasteful legacy of Albertans. From campfire rings to giant cities, from sunken gas lines to robotic space probes and from petroglyphs to computer chips, Albertans are leaving a sediment of their comings and goings on the plains and forests of this province. It may well be the task of their grandchildren or their grandchildren's children to discover, interpret and judge this legacy as palaeontologists and geologists have begun to do for the creatures and the land before us.

Located deep in the Alberta badlands, the Royal Tyrrell Museum of Palaeontology at Drumheller provides the world a unique opportunity to restore the memory of fabled lands and creatures.

RECOMMENDED READINGS

The following books are recommended by the Royal Tyrrell Museum of Palaeontology for those wishing to learn more about Alberta's past, and about its dinosaurs, geology and palaeontology in general.

Geology

Beaty, C. *The Landscapes of Southern Alberta: A Regional Geomorphology.* Lethbridge: University of Lethbridge Printing Services, 1984.

Cooper, J.D., et al. *A Trip Through Time.* Columbus: Merrill Publishing, 1990.

Godfrey, J.D., ed. *Edmonton Beneath Our Feet: A Guide to the Geology of the Edmonton Region.* Edmonton: Edmonton Geological Society, 1993.

Hartmann, W.K., and R. Miller. *The History of Earth.* New York: Workman Publishing, 1991.

Jackson, L.E., and M.C. Wilson, eds. *Geology of the Calgary Area.* Calgary: Canadian Society of Petroleum Geologists, 1987.

Mossop, G., ed. *Geological Atlas of the Western Canadian Sedimentary Basin.* Calgary: Canadian Society of Petroleum Geologists, 1994.

Nelson, S.J. *The Face of Time.* Calgary: Alberta Society of Petroleum Geologists, 1970.

Ricketts, B.D., ed. *Western Canada Sedimentary Basin: A Case History.* Calgary: Canadian Society of Petroleum Geologists, 1989.

Storer, J. *Geological History of Saskatchewan.* Regina: Government of Saskatchewan, 1989.

Wicander, R., and J.S. Monroe. *Historical Geology: Evolution of the Earth and Life Through Time.* Minneapolis/St. Paul: West Publishing Company, 1993.

Yorath, C.J. *Where Terranes Collide.* Vancouver: Orca Book Publishers, 1990.

Palaeontology

Bakker, R.T. *The Dinosaur Heresies.* New York: William Morrow and Co. Inc., 1986.

Currie, P.J., and J. Sovak. *The Flying Dinosaurs.* Red Deer: Red Deer College Press, 1991.

Cvancara, A.M. *Sleuthing Fossils: The Art of Investigating Past Life.* Toronto: John Wiley & Sons Inc., 1990.

Halstead, L.B. *The Search for the Past: Fossils, Rocks, Tracks and Trails: The Search for the Origin of Life.* New York: Doubleday & Company, 1982.

Lewin, R. *Thread of Life: The Smithsonian Looks at Evolution.* Washington: Smithsonian Books, 1982.

Norman, D. *The Illustrated Encyclopedia of Dinosaurs.* New York: Crescent Books, 1985.

Norman, D. *The Prehistoric World of the Dinosaur.* Leicester: Magna, 1989.

Reader, J. *The Rise of Life.* New York: Alfred A. Knopf, 1986.

Reid, M. and J. Sovak. *The Last Great Dinosaurs.* Red Deer: Red Deer College Press, 1990.

Russell, D.A. *A Vanished World.* Ottawa: National Museum of Natural Sciences; and Edmonton: Hurtig Publishers, 1977.

Russell, D.A. *An Odyssey in Time: The Dinosaurs of North America.* Toronto: University of Toronto Press, 1989.

Sternberg, C.H. *Hunting Dinosaurs in the Badlands of the Red Deer River, Alberta, Canada.* Edmonton: NeWest Press, 1985.

INDEX